My Life as a Dog

My Life as a Dog

by Moose, who
portrays TV's Eddie

with Brian Hargrove

HarperEntertainment
An Imprint of HarperCollins*Publishers*

Moose and I would both like to dedicate this book to our moms—who taught us that we could do anything if we just set our minds to it.

HarperEntertainment books may be purchased for educational, business, or sales promotional use. For information please write: Special Markets Department, HarperCollins Publishers Inc., 10 East 53rd Street, New York, NY 10022–5299.

FIRST EDITION

Designed by Jeannette Jacobs and Susan Sanguily

Library of Congress Cataloging-in-Publication Data has been applied for.

ISBN 0-06-105172-1
00 01 02 03 04 10 9 8 7 6 5 4 3 2 1

Acknowledgments

From Mathilde de Cagny—

I would like to dedicate this book to Gary and Barbara Gero, who welcomed me into the business and, more important, into their family. All my gratitude to Gwen Myers for taking me under her wing. I can't thank Roger Schumacher enough for teaching me the art of being a Trainer and for giving me the opportunity to work on *Frasier*. Thanks to Cathy Morrison, who gave me Moose—the dog responsible for some of the greatest … and worst moments of my life. Moose is no picnic. To all the veterinarians who have given Moose good care and kept him healthy—Drs. Jim and Linda Peddie, Dr. David Neilsen and all the staff at Pet Medical Center. To Lori DeHoog, for Moose's last-minute trims. To the cast of *Frasier*, thank you for being good sports and putting up with Moose and me. Peter Casey, David Angell & David Lee, who have been so helpful. Had it not been for their creating the character of Eddie, all this would not have been possible. Marshal Coben, for his support. Paramount Television, for their help. Paul Hargrave, for always having an answer. Brigit Binns, for her excellent advice, and for introducing us to Maureen and Eric Lasher. To Susan Sanguily and Allison McCabe of HarperCollins for their guidance. Brian Hargrove for finding the voice of Moose; your work exceeded my expectations. My future husband, Michael Halberg, for his many contributions and support. To Moose, a master of his Craft. I love you.

From Moose—

I would like to thank—no one, I did it all myself. Okay, okay. I would like to thank Mathilde de Cagny, without whom this book never would have been written because I would not be the dog I am today. Larry Ashmead, because he showed a brainy prescience, a sixth sense, and an intuitive understanding of the taste of the American public. And Brian Hargrove for his opposable thumbs.

From Brian Hargrove—

I would like to thank David Hyde Pierce, John Mahoney, Jane Leeves, Peri Gilpin, and Kelsey Grammer for helping to kick-start the book. Connie Thise and Cathy Morrison for taking the time to interview with me. Allison McCabe at HarperCollins, who's been a delight to work with. Maureen Lasher for her insight and editing skills, and Candace Burnett for the same thing. Emma and Mabel because nothing beats real life experience. And Moose, because I guess I have to. And finally, Mathilde de Cagny—Moose is right, without you this book never would have been written, thank you for choosing me to help him write it.

Contents

1. Who Am I Really, and What Makes Me Tick? 1

2. Humble Beginnings 13
   (or, How You Gonna Keep Me Down on the Farm After I've Seen *The Beverly Hillbillies*?)

3. My Stay at the Blacksmith's 23

4. Getting Out 25

5. I Oughta Be in Pictures 33

6. Go West, Young Puppy (or, Hurray for What?) 41

7. My Audition for the Television Show *Frasier* 49

8. A Letter to My Mom 53

9. She Said, He Said 59

10. The *Frasier* Chronicles 65

11. The Stare 75

12. Player Pooch 77

13. My Incredible Range 83

14. My Private Life 87

15. Celebrity Encounters of the Third Kind 95

16. The Tabloids: Truth or Fiction? 103

17. Dear Moose 113

18. My Way 123

1. Who Am I Really, and What Makes Me Tick?

t was lunchtime on the *Frasier* set—time in between the morning rehearsals and the producer's run-through. We were in the green room, the common area where actors traditionally hang out together. It isn't really green, it's just called the green room because of hundreds and hundreds of years of theatrical tradition. Why that applies to television I have no idea. There's so much about this business I still don't understand.

Most of the cast was just kicking back, having a smoke (not me, I've quit), flipping through the trades, and making phone calls to their agents. I, of course, was working on my book. The deadline was in a few weeks and the publisher wouldn't stop nagging me about it. I kept telling them it was almost done, but I had lied. Yeah, like I'm the first author to ever do that.

I hadn't written word one because I didn't know how to begin. I wanted to write this autobiography for three reasons. One, I wanted to put an end to the vicious rumors about me. Two, America had been clamoring for my story for years. And three, I had already spent the advance. Yeah, like I'm the first author to ever do that, either.

But, what to say, what to say? I didn't know what to say. How could I get a perspective on myself? Then it occurred to me. Why not ask my nearest and dearest, a.k.a. my fellow cast members? So, while we were on a small break and I had them all together, I took this opportunity to ask John Mahoney, Jane Leeves, Peri Gilpin, David Hyde Pierce, and Kelsey Grammer a few questions.

Me   Thank you all for being here.

Kelsey We have no choice. We're stuck here with you until rehearsal is over.

Me   Right. I don't have much time then, so I'm just going to get right down to the point. You know I'm writing this book.

Peri   Oh, God.

John   Not the damn book again.

David Moose has a book deal?

MOOSE-ISM

THE ONLY GOOD CAT IS A DEAD CAT.

Jane   Would you all just be quiet and let him finish?

Me   Thank you, Jane.

Jane   You just better not blow it for the rest of us, you silly mutt. I've got memoirs too you know.

David Moose has a book deal?

Me   Look, I'm just going to ask you some questions about my favorite subject.

Peri   Let me guess. You.

Me   Right.

Kelsey   Surprise, surprise.

Me   Do you mind doing this?

Kelsey   Oh, no.

John   Be delighted.

Peri   Absolutely.

Jane   Go ahead, ask us anything.

David   I don't have a book deal.

Me   All right. I thought I'd start with a general question, and then we'd get down to specifics. So, first question. *What color do I remind you of and why?*

David   Brown, because you are so full of—

Jane   Purple—the regal color of kings.

Peri   Yellow. The color of the sun.

David   He must have something on the girls.

John   Electric blue. Sometimes you short-circuit, and you don't know whether to wag your tail or pee on a chair. It's like your mind splatters.

Me   Kels?

Kelsey   I hate it when you call me Kels.

Me   Just answer the question.

Kelsey All right, it's a tough one. Let me see. I'm getting a washed-out canvas. A hazy, dreamlike, nightmarish vision . . .

Me Thank you. That's plenty.

Kelsey I haven't finished.

Me Yes, you have. Now to the show. *What are the differences between me and the character I play on TV?*

Jane Well, I think Eddie is very accepting of others. You, however, Moose, do not suffer fools easily.

John And I'd say that on TV you are warm and loveable to everyone, while the real you is just working for treats. But, both on TV and in life, you're a one person dog–on TV, it's Martin, in real life, it's your trainer, Mathilde.

David You're left-handed, and Eddie doesn't smoke.

Me I quit smoking.

David Yeah, right. Smell your breath, nicotine paws.

Kelsey The character you play on TV is a *good* dog.

Me (To Kelsey) You don't get to answer if you don't take this seriously.

Kelsey I am serious.

Me Fine. Peri?

Peri Well, of course, there's the physical difference. You always wear contacts on stage and a skullcap to hide your luxurious curls. And there's that whole beer and pretzel thing you bring to the character of Eddie.

Me	Yeah. I'm really more of a champagne and caviar kind of guy.
John	Are you going to write that?
Me	Maybe.
John	People will believe anything.
Me	Next question. *What would* Frasier *be without me?*
Peri	Nothing.
Kelsey	A lot funnier.
Me	(Sigh) Jane?
Jane	Like French fries without ketchup.
David	Flealess.
John	On his second or third pilot by now. Oh, you meant the show? I thought you meant Kelsey.
Me	Okay. Next question. *Have you ever disagreed with how I've played a scene?*
Kelsey	Almost without exception.
John	Yes. The two times you bit me.
David	No, darling, you're always perfect.
Peri	Honestly, I've always been shocked and stunned with the life and the realism, the universality, the dazzling showmanship you bring to each and every scene.
John	He really must have something on Peri.
Jane	I'm confused by your choices.

Me   Really?

Jane   But that's the point, isn't it? It's what makes you such an exciting performer.

Me   Well, yeah. *Then what separates me from other canine performers you've seen?*

Kelsey I work with you.

Me   You know you're beginning to get on my nerves.

Kelsey Well, turnabout is fair play.

David   You're shorter than Lassie. You're shorter than Rin Tin Tin. Basically, you're just short.

John   The speed that you work. Sometimes I'm amazed at how fast you pick things up.

Peri   Your thirst for life.

Jane   You're not afraid to look like an ass. You make strong choices and smells.

Me   I'm sorry about that. It's those darn doggy treats. This next one is a fill in the blank. *Moose, it always brings a smile to my face when I see you _____.*

Kelsey In your cage.

David   Asleep.

John   Are not in the next episode.

Peri   Come on guys, give him a break. Moose, it always makes me smile when you arrive with your entourage.

Jane   Yeah. I love the way you trot defiantly onto the set as if to say, "All right, give me your best shot and let's make 'em laugh."

Me   So far, Peri and Jane are giving the best answers.

MOOSE-ISM

IF YOUR BARK IS WORSE THAN YOUR BITE, YOU'RE NOT BITING HARD ENOUGH.

David   If you don't quit commenting on this, I'm leaving.

John   Ditto.

Me   Okay, fine. *I've been described as one of the greatest dog performers in show business; how would you describe me?*

David   Short.

Kelsey   As. . . one. . . of. . . the greatest dog performers in show business.

Jane   As *the* greatest dog performer. You're able to bring complexity and humor to an otherwise standard character—a dog.

Peri   I'll agree with that. As *the* greatest.

John   A little past your prime. I know the feeling.

Me   *And of all my incredible performances on* Frasier, *what is your favorite?*

Jane   Wow, that's tough. I would have to say, the show where you were depressed because you couldn't find your Barbie—I really felt your pain.

Kelsey I have two. The one when I attempted to lure you into jumping off the balcony with that tennis ball.

Me Yeah, real funny. Ha ha.

Kelsey Well, the look you gave me was hilarious. And my other favorite was when you had to wear the cone. I wanted you to be quieter, and instead they gave you a megaphone.

Me I don't remember that episode. Why was I so funny in that one?

Kelsey You looked ridiculous.

John I liked you in last year's Christmas episode, when the family was pretending to be Jewish. (There was a really good reason.) But you weren't in on the ruse yet, and you came running out in your little Christmas outfit, realized the circumstances, and got the hell out of there. Well, you made a great entrance, got your applause, and made a perfectly timed exit.

Me Thank you.

John You're welcome.

David I loved your character work in the dead seal episode. You really looked like a seal.

Me That *was* a seal.

David Oh. Ick.

Peri I love the way you sing the theme song.

Kelsey That's me.

Peri Oh. It sounds like Moose.

Me   *If you could wish anything for me, what would it be?*

Jane   Inner peace.

Kelsey   Early retirement.

David   A shorter tongue.

John   Your own show.

Peri   A great bitch to spend your golden years with.

Me   *If I told you that you are my favorite actor on the show, how would that make you feel?*

David   Dirty.

John   You must be mistaking me for someone else in the cast.

Peri   That kind of buttering up stopped working years ago, Moose.

Kelsey   I'd know that you'd said that to all the other actors on the show, so I'm not buying it.

Jane   I'd be humbled.

Me   *What does your character feel about Eddie?* Let's start with you, Jane, right now I really do like you best.

Peri   Hey.

Me   Along with Peri.

David   That's it, I'm out of here.

John   Yep, me too.

Me   Guys, come on, I'm begging you. As a professional.

Jane   Daphne thinks he's smelly and annoying, but deep down she adores him.

David Niles thinks that he's small and grubby, but knows how to wear a hat.

Peri It takes a bit of method acting on my part (because I love you so much), but Roz is hardly aware of Eddie.

John Martin worships the ground Eddie walks on. He loves him more than anything else in the world.

Me Including his own kids?

John In a different way. Eddie has always understood Martin more than his children have.

Kelsey Yeah. Frasier thinks that you are a warm and wonderful companion for his dad. You are indispensable to him.

Me Okay. Last question, and this will really help me with my book. *Who am I, and what makes me tick?*

David You're Laurence Olivier in a hair shirt. But what's this about ticks?

Kelsey You're a vicious little eating machine. And what makes you tick? Doggy treats.

John You're the reincarnation of Rin Tin Tin. And you have an incredible ambition to outshine him. It must be because of your height.

Jane You're a complicated little fellow, with a crusty exterior and a heart of gold. Like the rest of us though, you're just trying to make a buck.

Peri You're really John Mahoney in a dog suit.

At that moment, Marc Sturdivant, the second AD—assistant director—came into the green room to announce that it was time for the producer's run through. I've never seen the cast so eager to get back to rehearsal. I thanked them for their help and ran to get Mathilde, my person. She likes to have me on the leash when we go on stage. It makes her feel like she's more in control. As I made my way down to the stage, I couldn't help but reflect on the cast, and all I could think was . . .

. . . petty, petty, petty, they're mean-spirited and bitter. It's clear they are all jealous of my talent and me. And I know why. They all hoped that *Frasier* would be about them and their little characters, but it's been clear from the get go that I was the break-out star.

When the show first went on the air, Warren Littlefield, president of NBC at the time, called and asked me if I wanted them to change the name of the show to *Eddie!*, because he was so clearly the most interesting character. But I told him no. Since America first got to know the show as *Frasier*, I didn't want to confuse anyone, and besides, it would upset Kelsey. I told Warren that as long as I continued to make one dollar more per episode than anyone else in the cast, I would be satisfied. Everyone knows that I'm the real reason America watches.

MOOSE-ISM

HE WHO LEARNS FAST, GETS FEWER TREATS.

But believe me. I don't blame the cast for their resentment. And I don't harbor any ill will toward them. I love them all. Without them there, supporting me every week, I couldn't shine. Without their monotonous stories and endless chatter, my glorious entrances and special moments might not stand out as much as they do. I need the supporting cast. They are the wind beneath my wings.

But enough about them. Let's get back to me.

What does make me tick? What's it really like to be me? How did I get here, and why am I so . . . me?

2. Humble Beginnings

(or, How You Gonna Keep Me Down on the Farm After I've Seen *The Beverly Hillbillies?*)

I was born on a freezing cold, rainy night, which was peculiarly strange for Florida. The town: Weirsdale. The year: 1990. It's been said that I act like I'm God's gift to the canine world. Well, I *was* born in a barn, it *was* December 24th, there *was* a bright star in the sky, and there was no *room* anywhere else…you do the math.

My mother delivered a litter of four puppies. I was the last one out——the runt. It's typical for the runt to be the smallest of the bunch, but in my case, I was the biggest. And since I was as big as a moose, that's what they named me—Moose. Hey, we were in Florida, it ain't exactly Noel Coward territory. And, actually, it worked out much better in the long run. They had planned to name me Petunia.

They say guys are always trying to return to the womb. Why? What I remember about the womb was that it was dark, it was crowded, and I was way in the back. Legs, paws, and newly forming puppy dog tails were constantly in my face, and I couldn't wait to escape. A theme I would revisit for the rest of my life.

When I did finally come out, I couldn't open my eyes, or hear a thing. I was cold and hungry. I knew there had to be food some-where, but I was hunting for it blind, and my brothers and sisters kept pushing me out of the way. Finally, I piled over the others, using my size to knock the little ones out of the way until I found my moth-er's milk. It was in that moment that I learned the most important les-son of my whole life:

Never hesitate to throw your weight around if you have to.

It's an important lesson, and I hope that if you take anything from this book, you will take that.

Unlike most, I remember every detail of my childhood from the moment I was born. But until I could see, life was pretty boring. Sleep and eat. Sleep and eat. Sometimes I would just eat in my sleep. My mom was great, though. She would feed us, and clean us, and growl at any strangers that came by to stare. Finally, I began to open

MOOSE-ISM

IT'S BETTER TO SNIFF THAN TO BE SNIFFED.

my eyes, no small feat for a puppy. It took me almost twenty-two hours. Then I tried walking around, which was kind of like riding a bicycle, without the bike. And then I came into my sense of smell.

For a dog, this was both a blessing and a curse. The blessing was that our sense of smell is about a hundred times stronger than a person's is, and we use this sense of smell the way people use their eyes. The curse was that we were in a barn with horses and cows. The smell could peel paint off a barn. I mean it was enough to make me want to give up eating hamburger, and I hadn't even tried it yet. Fortunately, the weather turned even colder and we couldn't stay outside anymore, so they put us in a room off the kitchen.

I realized then that I was not a free dog. I was a prisoner. The room off the kitchen had high walls and a scary-looking gate at the door. They would let my mom come and go as she pleased—she just jumped over the gate—but they made the rest of us stay in this tiny little room and do our business on newspaper. As if that wasn't humiliating enough, they began to take the newspaper away a little bit at a time, so that the area became smaller and smaller. Finally, they removed the newspaper altogether, so we would have to wait to go to the bathroom outside. You know how hard it is to pee when the temperature is below freezing? It's hard, let me tell you. But this was when I saw my first chance to escape.

We went outside to "use the newspaper," and when no one was looking, I snuck through a hole underneath the house. Free at last, I thought. Free at last. No I wasn't, I was free and *lost*.

It was dark under the house, and once I got under there, I couldn't find my way out. I could hear footsteps above me, but I didn't know where in the house they were coming from. I began to panic and, I'll be honest, I may have whimpered . . . a little. But, I was determined not to be scared.

That was when I saw my first cat. It looked like an overgrown rat, and I didn't even know what a rat was then. It was furry and white, with green slits for eyes. I was curious, so I went behind it, to sniff its butt, because that's what you're supposed to do when you meet a fellow creature from the animal kingdom. Why? I don't know. But then, you people kiss on the lips. Go figure.

Anyway, out of the blue, for no reason whatsoever, the cat smacked me on the nose! And it hurt! A lot! This was not a thing I wanted to be friends with. In fact, I wanted to be as far away from this cat as caninely possible.

So, I ran away in the other direction. But suddenly, the cat was in front of me. Smack. It hit me again! No matter which way I turned, the cat was there smacking me. Cats are fast. And this one was playing me like a giant ball of string. I yelped–not because I was scared, mind you, but because crying, no matter how sissifying, was the only thing to do in this particular circumstance.

And thank God I did. 'Cause my mother heard my pleas, and appeared out of nowhere, and scared the bejezuz out of that cat. It was hilarious. She (it could have been a he, but I've always thought all cats were female) took off like someone had set her tail on fire. And my mother, my wonderful mother, my mother the superhero, picked me up by the scruff of my neck and whisked me away to safety, after she smacked me and threatened to kill me if I ever got into danger like that again. Then she grounded me for the rest of the month.

It was worth it though, because that's when I developed my lifelong love of cats. I know it's typical for dogs to hate cats. But I don't. I love them. I love to chase them, and torment them, and grab them with my teeth. I love to bark at them, and run them up trees, or scare them into traffic. Which brings me to the second most important lesson of my life:

Cats are delicious.
Either as a snack or main course, depending on the size of the cat.

This is also an important lesson, and I hope that if you get anything else out of this book, you will get that.

Later that day, after my mother had left us to gather food and toys from other parts of the house, I celebrated with my brothers and sisters. And since my mother wasn't there, I regaled them with my victorious defeat of our feline foe. How I wrestled it to the ground until it begged for mercy, and swore it would never touch another canine again. Okay, I may have exaggerated a little, but I was eight weeks old, give me a break.

Eight weeks old. How can I forget that period in my life? When my family was torn apart. I didn't realize what was happening at first. About a week before my brothers and sisters began to disappear, all these different people came into the kitchen and stared at us over the pen. Naturally, we would yelp and paw the pen to try and get their attention. They would take one of us out, make cooing noises and play with us, and then put us back, and take another. One day I went out to play, and when I came back my sister Mabel wasn't there. No good-bye or nothing. Jeesh.

I asked my mother what was going on, but she was too depressed to discuss it. The next day, Marlboro disappeared and then so did Mateo, until it was just me and Mom left. My mother finally explained that they had gone to nice families because Connie and Sam This could only afford to keep one of us. Naturally they chose me. I guess it's always been clear, even when I was just a cute little puppy, that I was special. But special for what?

I never fit in. Not really. Certainly, not on a farm in podunk Florida. See, the Thises (and no, I don't know how to pronounce it, either) bred dogs to hunt in competitions. They would set up a series of agility courses and the dogs would run the courses while trying to hunt game. Like I was going to spend my life doing that.

But what was I going to do? I had no schooling. I wasn't a big reader. I was too short for the military. And the only other working dogs I had heard about chased sheep. For a while, I barked with an English accent for no reason whatsoever except to show that I was different. I guess I was screaming for attention. Until one day, I found my calling.

I had taken another Tupperware chew toy out of the drawer when Connie wasn't looking, and I was on my way to my secret hiding place behind the chair in the den, when I first noticed the television.

Don't get me wrong, I had seen the television before. In fact, it was on almost all the time at our house. I used to think Americans watched too much of it, but I've since changed that tune. Now, I think Americans don't watch enough television. They should take televisions to work. Watch them in their cars, keep them in churches. Television is an important part of our culture and we should embrace it happily. Come on, people, I gotta eat. But I digress.

What grabbed my attention on the television this particular day was a dog! A big, ugly, hound dog, living in this gigantic palace in the Hills of Beverly, somewhere in a place called California, home of swimming pools and movie stars. I set the Tupperware lid aside for a later treat, and watched the box.

I don't know what the show was, but there was a Jed, and a Jethro, a Granny, and an Ellie May. Plus, a big, ugly hunk of a bloodhound named Duke. Oh, all the actors were good, but there was no doubt about it, that canine colossus was the star. Until that time, it had never occurred to me that dogs could be on television. I had seen wolves on the Discovery Channel. And of course, we owned the movie *101 Dalmatians*. But that was a cartoon. I didn't realize that a dog like me could star in his own television show.

In order to understand me completely, I think you need to know a little bit more about my breeding. I wish I could say that I come from a long line of actors, like the Barrymores—a famous theatrical family. But it just ain't so. The Reverend John Russell developed us in nineteenth century England (hence, the name Jack Russell—for you slow readers out there). We were bred to go into a fox's burrow and do what we had to do to get the foxes out. And because of that, my kind still have a tendency to hunt, or "go to ground" as they say in jaunty England, until we can snag our quarry—gopher, opossum, neighbor's cat, dirty sock, you name it.

Although we aren't British royalty (not officially, anyway), we are strong, healthy dogs, and we don't have the genetic defects that a lot of purebred dogs have, because basically, we'll sleep with anybody. Well, almost anybody. You won't find us inbreeding, except perhaps some of my cousins in Appalachia.

According to the dog books, we're "working" terriers—demanding, willful, headstrong, smarter than hell, and we need lots of discipline and a firm hand. And I suppose that's true. Although, I say just give me everything I want, and you'll never have a problem.

My dad was a stud. I don't mean he was a sexy dog about town—that goes without saying. But, studding is how he made a living. He studded puppies. Not for show, mind you, as the American Kennel Club doesn't recognize us as a breed. (Hello?! What are they thinking?!) But at least you won't see any of us all dolled up and sashaying around the ring like a bunch of pansy contestants in a beauty pageant. Although if my mom had ever entered a beauty pageant, she would have won.

My mom was beautiful. I guess every kid thinks his mom is the most beautiful creature on the planet, but mine really was. She had a brown and white face, with a black circle around her left eye. She had a long, graceful, white body, and the most luxurious tail. Before she met my dad, she was a model. She frequently appeared in grocery store circulars advertising specials on dog foods. But she chose her family over her career. I guess that's why I had acting in my blood.

I didn't know much about the "biz they call show," so I was determined to learn as much as I could. Any time someone turned on the TV, I was there. Watching, learning. I even figured out how to use the remote, to the point where Connie thought there was something wrong with the television because it kept turning on mysteriously.

When I discovered cable, I was able to see the two greatest canine actors of all time: Rin Tin Tin, voted most popular star in America in 1925, and Lassie, the smartest dog in show business, with an IQ well above most people's. Lassie and Rin Tin Tin each had their own style. Lassie was caring and gentle as she guided Timmy through life. While Rinny—I call him Rinny for short, like his sidekick did in the movies—Rinny was more heroic. Always coming to the rescue, and succeeding through sheer bravery.

Early on I decided, mainly because of my size, that I would probably have a better chance breaking into the business as a comic actor. I've always been a practical puppy, and Hollywood is known for its typecasting. Meaning they limit you according to your looks. For instance, Mr. Ed never got to play anything other than a horse.

In order to develop my natural and immense talent for comedy (my comedy chops, as they say in the industry), I studied the Benji movies, and Charlie in *The Absentminded Professor*. But, believe it or not, the actor who taught me the most was Scooby Doo. His timing was exquisite, and he would do some of the funniest takes to the camera. It wasn't his fault that the plots were always the same, and he had to play the scaredy-cat.

I would watch my heroes on television, and then try to repeat what they did by putting on little skits for the barnyard animals. They would look at me like I was an idiot. No imagination. And don't let anybody tell you any differently. Horses are dumb, cows have no sense of humor, and chickens are delicious. Okay, I accidentally ate a few while I was working on a monologue from *Julius Caesar*. *Et tu, Moosé?*

Since I was a flop with the barnyard animals, I decided to try out my newfound skills on Connie. I pretended I hurt my paw, and walked with a limp for several days. But that was a stupid idea 'cause I ended up at the vet, who discovered I was due for a shot.

MOOSE-ISM

A CAT IS A WONDERFUL THING TO WASTE.

So, after a while, I would just practice my skills alone, doing death scenes on the second floor landing, and falling down flights of stairs as if I had been shot. Connie would come running out of the kitchen to see if I was okay, and I would just laugh and laugh. She'd be so mad.

Sometimes, I'd create little scenarios about how robbers had tied and bound us all under the stairs and, like Rinny, it was up to me to rescue us. I had to gnaw through the cords so we could all escape. The problem was I had to substitute household props for the real thing, and I'd usually get yelled at, for chewing the cord of the blind, or scratching a hole though the screen door so I could get out of the house to chase the bad guys. Connie thought I was just misbehaving, but I wasn't: I was acting.

Frequently, she'd lock me in my crate for what she called my incessant barking. But I wasn't barking, I was vocalizing. This became a never-ending circle. Me getting into trouble, Connie yelling and putting me in my crate.

They just didn't understand me—they seldom do when you're an artist. (This continues to haunt me even now that I'm an international star. But again, I digress.) Connie and Sam thought I was destroying their house for no reason, when actually I was crying out for a decent acting coach. What I needed was to train with someone. A teacher who could help me work on my craft. But where the hell was I going to find someone like that on a farm? It wasn't that I didn't like Sam and Connie—they were wonderful, caring human beings—but they were simple people who didn't know anything about show business, and show business was my destiny.

I used to dream that they would hold a talent contest, and I would enter it, and a talent scout would see me, and recognize my star quality. Or that Francis Ford Coppola would come to town scouting the location for his next movie, and I would be discovered peeing on a hydrant. Little did I know that one day my dream would come true—but not before Sam and Connie had given me to a blacksmith! *A blacksmith!?*

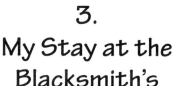

3.
My Stay at the
Blacksmith's

How was my stay at the blacksmith's? Well, I got rid of his favorite cat. I started a small fire while he wasn't looking. I let several of the horses loose. I jumped on the counter and ate his lunch. It was a ham sandwich. I don't even like ham.

Two days, fifteen hours, twenty-three minutes, and twelve seconds later, the blacksmith gave me back.

4.
Getting Out

After the blacksmith, I was right back where I started, with Connie and Sam and their kids. All of whom I loved, and they loved me, too. How could they not? But that didn't stop them from holding me back. What about my career? What about my dreams? They didn't care.

I knew I was ready. My training had been going well. Even the cows were laughing at my pratfalls. But my acting chops were limited. I was self-taught, and you can only teach yourself so much. I had to get out of there. But how?

As long as I remained nice and friendly, the perfect little puppy, not only would it have been boring, I knew they would never let me go. So I decided to challenge. Everything and everybody. I would act extremely selfish—like a teenager or a juvenile delinquent. I would be irksome and annoying, maddening and irritating, exasperating and infuriating. In short, I would be a Jack Russell terrier.

When I think of all the things I did to that poor family, I'm a little embarrassed. I didn't think about consequences. I didn't think about the effect I was having on the others around me. All I thought about was myself.

Oh, boy, the things we do when we are young. I don't know about you, but I've blocked out many of the mistakes of my past. I've lost them in a haze of deliberate forgetfulness. And I'm really glad I'm not an elephant.

For this to be an honest account of my life, warts and all, I had to talk to Connie Thise in Florida. I needed to know what she remembered about me. What it was like to have an *über*-star grow up in your home. So, I called her up—thank God for push-button phones.

Connie   Hello?

Me   Connie, how are you? It's Moose.

Connie   Moose who?

Me   Eddie from *Frasier*?

Connie   Oh, *that* Moose.

(For some reason, she took a very long pause.)

Connie   How are you, Moose?

Me   I'm good, Connie.

Connie   You don't want to move back in, do you?

Me   No, Connie, I'm doing fine on my own.

Connie   Oh. Well, in that case, what can I do for you, Moose?

Me   I'm writing a book, and I'm having a little trouble remembering what I was like as a puppy.

Connie   You were rotten from the very beginning.

Me   (Okay, there's a wart.) But Connie, that's not true. Until I decided I wanted to pursue an acting career, I was a perfectly behaved puppy.

Connie   You were a whiner from day one. Whine, whine, whine. You were especially loud when you were hungry. If we didn't feed you at the exact same time every day, you'd start your whining. I thought you'd never shut up.

Me   Well, I suppose even as a child I could be pretty demanding.

Connie   Demanding? Ha! You were a tyrant. But it meant you got carried around a lot. That's why you're so spoiled.

Me   Wait a minute, Connie, if I was so rotten, why didn't you keep one of my brothers or sisters instead of me?

Connie   Nobody wanted you. The other three were chosen right away. But not you. No sir. You just kept hanging around. And then the kids got pretty attached to you. I even grew a little attached to you.

Me   Aha. You admit it. So you did like me!

Connie   Did you hear me? Only a *little* attached! I liked you . . . sometimes. You were obnoxious, but you were still a puppy. And puppies have that effect on people. They're just so darn adorable.

Me   So, what you're saying is that I was an adorable puppy?

Connie   No, you were a menace. You would mess in your crate, and stomp all in it, and then you'd chew right through the bars. We went through two crates for you. Finally we just gave up and let you ruin the rest of the house.

Me   Oh, well, that must have been after I came back from the blacksmith. There was a reason I was behaving like that.

Connie Oh, no, that was when you were just a puppy. After you came back from the blacksmith, you were much worse. I'd like to say you were in your terrible twos, because you were two, but for a dog that's fourteen and you should have known better. You would chew doors, eat telephone wires, bite the legs of the dining room table, rip apart the couch and spit upon the stereo speakers. You even lifted your leg on Sam's favorite chair. And remember the neighbor's cattle?

Me   Well, yeah, a little.

Connie A little?! Well, maybe this will jog your memory. You used to go to their pasture, and roll in a big fresh pile of cow dung, and then come back and rub all over my living room carpet and white sofa. Get the picture now?

MOOSE-ISM

VOMIT IS NATURE'S DESSERT.

Me Yeah. But, see, that was all part of my master plan. I wanted you to let me go.

Connie Let you go? Who could keep you? You were constantly on the move. Every time I'd open the door, you'd run out to terrorize every animal in the neighborhood. I mean, you were fine with the two other dogs in our house, the Doberman and his mother. You even got along with the cats, as long as they were inside the house. But outside, even they were fair game. The poor neighbor's cat spent half her time up a pine tree in their front yard. You know, after you left, the neighbors called and thanked us for getting rid of you. They were that relieved. They wept with joy.

Me Well, they say that a prophet is never recognized in his own hometown. You just didn't understand me, that's all. And you wanted me to go into the family business. You were angry. That's understandable. I forgive you.

Connie What family business?

Me You bred dogs to hunt in competitions—

Connie Have you lost your mind? I worked for a vet. We bred Jack Russells for pleasure. We enjoyed it—training them, and showing them. But you ruined it for us. We don't breed dogs anymore.

Me But, I remember you took me to the terrier trials and had me run the races. We did steeplechases, and flat races.

Connie You seemed to enjoy it, but you didn't do very well. You were too young, and I wasn't racing you every day. I couldn't enter you in a lot of the competitions, because you were too tall for breed standards.

Me (Hopefully) But I won ribbons.

Connie You came in third. And there were only two others in your event.

Me Oh, my God. I was nothing but a big, fat loser.

Connie Yes, you were. Thanks for calling, Moose.

Me That's it. You're just going to leave me like this.

Connie Oh. Don't feel bad, honey, you weren't cut out to be a farm dog. If you had stayed with us, chances are your life would have been cut short. The Randalls wanted to put Drano in your food. The Kirbys tried to run you over with their tractor, using those really nasty plowing blades, too. And I heard the Husseys were getting ready to—

Me   Stop! Stop! I get the idea; you decided to find me another home to save my life.

Connie Oh, no, that wasn't it at all. One morning, I was having my morning coffee in the breakfast nook, when I looked out the window and saw you tormenting Tommy.

Me   The Morgan gelding? I wasn't tormenting him. We were just having fun.

Connie You had latched on to his tail, and you were hanging three or four feet off the ground. Tommy was running all around the yard kicking and screaming, and you were just hanging on for the ride.

Me   Well, maybe I was having more fun than he was.

Connie You almost pulled all the hair out of that poor horse's tail. That, and the fact that you had dug a hole through the wall of the upstairs bathroom, made it clear to us you finally had to go. When Sam saw that, he was furious. I was given an ultimatum—you or him.

Me   And you chose him? I'll bet you're sorry now.

Connie Oh, yes, I'm miserable. Why don't you come back and I'll have the Randalls bring over some Drano doggy treats.

Me   Okay, not that miserable. Guess I was lucky that Cathy Morrison was in the clinic the next day.

Connie   Darn tootin'. She was working for that Birds and Animals Unlimited company, and I figured if they could handle show-biz dogs they could handle you.

Me   But is it true that you just handed me to Cathy, told her you were moving to Zimbabwe and would be living in a thatched hut with no postal address?

Connie   Well, I may have exaggerated a little. But, Moose, I would have done anything to get rid of you. You were working my every last nerve.

Me   Wow. You know, Connie, you've been a little rough on me today. I can't help wondering if you aren't a little jealous of my success.

Connie   Not in the least. I'm thrilled that you moved to L.A., we all are. That's almost three thousand miles away. . . . Oh, you meant the star stuff. We're happy about that too. We didn't realize how different you were. We thought you were just difficult, and headstrong, and obnoxious, and smelly, and—

Me   —And special.

Connie   Yes you are, honey. You're special. That was on my list . . . somewhere.

Me   And you're special too. After all, I lived with you before I was discovered. That makes you special to all my fans.

Connie   Well, I'm so glad you called—now I can sleep tonight. Are we done? 'Cause I've got supper to get on. Not all of us eat in big fancy restaurants like you TV stars, you know.

Me   Just one more thing. How's Mom? I haven't seen her since I was hosting the Orlando Winter Pet Fest. I was so busy bragging about myself that day, I barely let her get a word in edgewise.

Connie Tag is great. She's my best friend. Probably the best dog I've ever had. She's not anything like you. She's strong willed, and definitely a Jack Russell, but without your, uh, sense of adventure. She's almost sixteen now, still in real good health. But she's getting up there. Sixteen is a hundred and twelve in people years, so she tires easily. But, when I look at her, I still see the young Tag, and she's as spry as ever. She's out in the garden right now helping Sam with the tomatoes.

Me Well, tell her I love her. I may be planning a trip out there soon.

Connie No. You can't. We're moving to Zimbabwe and we'll be living in a thatched hut with no postal address.

Me Okay, I won't come visit. I'll just call you every week.

Connie You do that, Moose. Take care. Bye.

(As she was hanging up, I could hear her yelling:)

Connie Sam, we've got to get an unlisted number . . .

I know she wanted me to hear her 'cause everyone knows a big television star like myself can trace an unlisted telephone number. She was always such a kidder.

After I spoke with Connie, I felt really good about myself. I think it's clear from that conversation that I was pretty darn special.

5.
I Oughta
Be in
Pictures

As you know from my telephone conversation with Connie, Cathy Morrison and I met at a veterinary clinic. A horrible place to meet under any circumstances, but in my case it worked to everyone's advantage.

Cathy worked for Birds and Animals Unlimited, which is a talent agency for the animal world. Although they work more like managers because they take way more than ten percent of your income.

Show Biz Bon Mot: Ten percent is standard for agents.

With Birds and Animals, you practically have to give them your soul to become a client. But after you do, they provide you with food, shelter, and, most importantly, treats. And they are absolutely necessary to get into show business, because you don't stand a chance on your own. You will just languish forever as an unknown. So the minute Cathy walked into the clinic on a routine checkup for one of her company's clients (actors), I knew this could be my lucky break. (I'd also heard the Husseys were planning my violent demise.) So I gave her my best come-hither look.

She noticed me (the come-hither look always works) and came over and started talking to Connie about me. Then, out of the blue,

Connie said, "You like him, you got him," and she gave Cathy my leash and walked away. Cathy asked her if she wouldn't like to think about it, or at least discuss it with her husband, but Connie said, "Nope," and ran out of that clinic like a wildebeest.

I knew from the beginning that Cathy and I were destined for each other. She was supposed to happen. She was the next step in God's universal plan for me. She was my destiny. She recognized how strong the force was within me. And I'm not saying that 'cause I just recently saw a rerun of *Star Wars*.

Cathy worshiped the ground I walked on. She called me a Holy Terrier. Or was it Holy Terror? I'm not sure. But she loved everything about me. So she decided to take me in and train me for film work on spec.

Show Biz Tidbit: *Train on spec* **means she would take the time and effort to train me with the hope I would become a huge star.**

Of course, in my case, it paid off.

I had that thing. That *je ne sais quoi* that talent scouts are looking for. The right look. The right personality.

What is the right look, you ask? Well, pretty isn't enough, let me tell you. You have to be unique. And I was unique, like no other Jack Russell she'd ever seen. Cathy described my look as a sort of planned dishevelment—grizzled but adorably cute. Who am I to argue with that?

The right personality? That is more nebulous. (Yes, nebulous: I can use a thesaurus with the best of 'em.) You can't be shy, but you can't be too eager to please. You have to be bold, but not obnoxious. You have to be cocky, but not mean. Fearless, but not aggressive. I was all these and more. So much more.

Cathy thought I was right for TV and film. And you should know something about Cathy: She has keen insight and a unique ability to pick out talent. She loved that I had a strong personality, and that I was very smart. Very, very, very, very, very smart. I might have been stubborn and a little difficult to train, but I could be bribed. She could pretty much get me to do anything for treats. I was, am, and always will be crazy for food. Or as one of the *Frasier* cast members put it, I'm a "treat whore."

You might think luck brought Cathy and me together, because when we met, I had all the specific traits she was looking for in a budding young actor. But I don't believe in luck. As Thomas Jefferson once said, "I find that the harder I work, the more luck I seem to have." Remember, I had done extensive research, watching the TV and cruising the Internet, so I knew how to position myself to attract attention.

Let this be a valuable lesson for all you struggling young actors out there. Your hard work will pay off if you're smart about it. Work on your acting, develop the right "personality," get a "look" that's right for you, and learn how to wag your tail when you need to.

When I first started my acting training with Cathy, she was working with the Animal Actors Showcase at Universal Studios Florida in Orlando. The show featured imitations of famous animals that Universal had bought the rights to. So most of the dogs in the show were look-alikes. Meaning they looked like Benji or Lassie or Beethoven. And they weren't very good. I mean, okay, they were fine as mimics go. But they were just copying what someone else had created. How hard could that have been? I wouldn't know. They wouldn't cast me in the show.

And yes, I was jealous. I could have acted circles around any one of those guys, but I wasn't the right "type." I didn't look like anybody famous, so I was "typed out."

Show Biz Lagniappe: *Typing out* **means you are not even given a chance to audition because of what you look like.**

It happens to animals, the same way it happens to people. And it's not fair. Who says Danny DeVito can't play a dashing leading man? And who says a pit bull can't play a friendly dog? Or that a dalmatian can't be the bad guy?

I've met quite a few nasty dalmatians in my day. But in the movies, those are the "cute" dogs. Especially the "oh, no, they're going to be made into a coat" dalmatians. I was rooting for Cruella.

Wait. What am I saying? That's just the bitterness talking. I'm sorry. Typecasting is a very upsetting thing for me. Why? Well, by Hollywood standards, I'm short. Too short to be a leading man. That's why I decided to become a character actor. It was not an easy decision to make. In my heart of hearts, I'm another James Dean.

I really *had* to concentrate on comedy. That's another lesson for you aspiring actors and actresses: Concentrate on your strengths. Cathy says that from the get go, I had comedy chops. She thought it was because of the extremely intense character of my personality. I'm intense. That's what made me so funny. And I so desperately wanted to do it professionally, so everyone could see just how funny I was.

Every day I would watch the Animal Actors Showcase patiently from the wings, marking my time until my chance would come. Someday I would be the draw. I would be the one people plunked down their hard-earned bucks to see. But back then I was a nobody.

A determined nobody, who took his acting lessons seriously. Think Harrison Ford before *Star Wars*.

As you know from some of my standout performances on *Frasier*, I'm a very physical dog. Well, I've always been that way. Very intense and very physical. Cathy noticed it right away. Whenever I would be around any other animals—chimps, pigs, owls—I'd bounce straight up off the ground like a kangaroo. So she capitalized on it. She took my instincts and turned them into craft.

A good acting teacher does that—recognizes your innate abilities and makes them stronger. Boy, I was lucky to find Cathy. And in this case, I do believe in luck. Most acting teachers just tear you down, trying to mold you into what they want you to be and not what you really are.

Since I was such a snappy, physical dog, my first trick or piece of business was what I call "the kangaroo jump." I leap straight up really high without even bending my legs. You've seen it many times on *Frasier*. Remember the episode that's about me trying to grab a bite of Frasier's muffin as he's trying to read the paper? That was the "kangaroo jump." Now you know.

Developing my physical side was not difficult. But one area I had problems with was the vocal. I was not much of a barker. That was because (and I can't believe I'm admitting this, but I promised you a no-holds-barred exposé, so I'm going to tell you) I was embarrassed by the sound of my own voice. I know, it's hard to believe now. Now, I'm the James Earl Jones of the animal kingdom. But back then, my voice sounded weak and reedy, almost feminine, because I didn't know how to use my vocal instrument properly. I wasn't using my diaphragm and getting enough breath when I barked.

Cathy and I tried exercise after exercise. But I just wasn't getting it. I've never been very good at working technically. I needed a reason to bark. Finally, Cathy came up with a brilliant idea. She knew how I hated farm animals, particularly pigs. And since we were at Universal, and they used pigs in some of their shows, she had me look at the pigs. And that's how I learned how to speak with distinction: by barking at pigs. If we were rehearsing a scene, and I needed to be reminded to bark from my diaphragm, I'd look at one of the pigs, and the sound would just come out naturally.

In Actor's Studio lingo, it's called substitution training. Using something that you know in order to get in touch with the proper emotion for a scene. Pigs always work for me. Now, whenever I need to bark, I just think of pigs and I'm there. (I hear Brando used the pig technique in *Streetcar*.)

Once Cathy had to break off our training while she went out of town to work on a movie. She had me stay at Universal where I shared a kennel with a much larger dog, a huge mastiff the size of a horse. The guy taking care of the kennels was new, and he didn't realize you are supposed to separate large and small dogs at feeding time. Otherwise the dominant dog might take the other dog's food. So I did. By the time Cathy returned, I was enormous, and the mastiff looked like a whippet with hair. I had eaten like a pig all week, not because I like pigs—we already know that I hate them—but because I wanted to emphasize to Cathy how disappointed I was that my training had stopped. She never left me alone again.

We lived together seven days a week, twenty-four hours a day, for over a year. Lucky Cathy. We would play all kinds of theater games. For instance, she'd put her bag full of delicious liver treats on the kitchen counter. Then while she was taking a shower or doing chores around the house, I was supposed to jump on the counter, and stuff myself silly until she discovered me. Then she would pretend to be mad, and she'd yell and scream while I ran away and hid.

Sometimes she would hide the bag of treats in different places—the cupboard, on top of the refrigerator, in the basement. And I was supposed to pretend I was 007 and find them. It was my favorite game. And she was really convincing as the enraged loser.

In a different game, she would give me a bath. Then, to help me with my character work, I was supposed to go out and roll in anything stinky I could find—rancid lawn clippings, raccoon excrement, raw sewage. By taking on those smells, I was able to change who I was. The only part I didn't understand about the game, and frankly hated, was that when I got back home Cathy would give me another bath. I thought it defeated the whole purpose. She said "it saved her den," whatever that means. I've yet to read Stanislavsky, but I'm sure it's a Chekhovian reference.

Other games we worked on were the arm-humping game, the who-peed-here-last game, and the rub-your-heinie-on-the-dining-room-rug game. There were way too many to go into, but you get the idea. I was a natural.

After about a year, I had the basics down, and Cathy felt that I had reached the point where I was ready to audition professionally. They were doing a commercial for the Louisiana State Lottery, and so Cathy sent them my picture. And, of course, I got it. The first job I was ever submitted on, I got. Well, the writing was on the wall, wasn't it? You don't get a much better sign that that.

My part in the commercial wasn't large. I, along with a bunch of other dogs from Birds and Animals, was supposed to chase a mailman through some sprinklers. Then I alone would be featured jumping over the hedge after him. This job was a cinch because, believe me, I didn't have to use any Actor's Studio substitutions to get in touch with my anger at the mailman—that was pure instinct. And I got to use the first piece of acting business I'd ever learned—the kangaroo jump.

Needless to say, it went swimmingly. They ran that commercial forever. The next thing I know they were sending me to Los Angeles to star in a new television show called *Frasier*. There was a relatively obscure actor from the television show *Cheers* named Kelsey Grammer in it too.

Hollywood had finally called. Who was I to say no?

6.
Go West, Young Puppy!
(or, Hurray for What?)

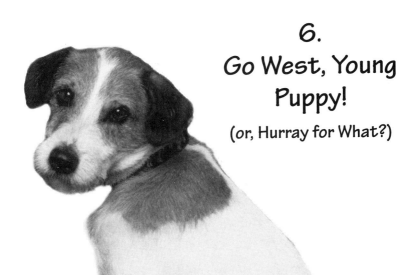

I was so excited. Finally, I was going to La La Land. This was going to be it, baby, the big time. I was following in Duke's pawprints—swimming pools, movie stars. My life was about to take a ride on the turnpike of fame, fortune, and success. And from now on, it was going to be first class all the way!

Can you tell I was a little excited?

We arrived at the airport in plenty of time. Too much time if you ask me; I like to arrive just as they are closing the doors of the plane. Well, at least I know that now. This was my first plane trip, so I was just happy to be at the airport.

Cathy had me on a leash; apparently there was some kind of stupid airport rule, dogs have to be on leashes. Just wait'll we rule the world. Anyway, as Cathy and I walked up to the counter, I was a little concerned because Cathy didn't have a ticket for herself, just one for me.

I became even more concerned when we didn't get in the line for First Class. Although I had never flown before, I still knew what First

Class was; we have an instinct about that sort of thing. (And when I say we, I mean stars, baby, stars.)

Well, we strolled right by the First Class line. And we strolled right by the line for (gulp) Coach. Instead, we went to the baggage line. The baggage line? What is this about, I wondered? And then I remembered. Oh, right, they needed to ship my crate. I had grown attached to it, and that Cathy was so considerate, always thinking of me.

Then a very strange thing happened. Cathy opened the door of my crate and told me to go inside. Maybe she's confused, I thought, because I'm going to be traveling in a seat like everyone else, right? Television stars don't fly in their crates. Then I realized: Silly, she's not sure if this is really my crate. That Cathy, she was always thinking of me. So, I decided to humor her and go in just to make sure. Yep, sure enough, it was my crate. *Bam!* She shut the door! And they put me on the conveyor belt with the rest of the luggage.

Okay, humoring is one thing, but someone had clearly made a serious mistake. I started screaming. I was going to Hollywood! They had called for me! I was going to a paradise where everything was pretty, and sunny, and people smiled all the time and everybody used cell phones and sat in Jacuzzis and ordered around their support staff. I was going to be a star! Tom Cruise doesn't travel like baggage!

But no one heard my pleas, or if they did, they ignored them. So my crate, with a very unhappy me, continued on down the conveyor belt until it went into a dark tunnel. After my eyes adjusted, I realized I was surrounded by thousands upon thousands of suitcases and boxes and golf bags and garment bags all traveling hither and thither (yes, hither and thither) on other conveyor belts. It might have been fun, like a ride at Disneyland, if the circumstances hadn't been so horrifying.

At one point, I passed a crated cat going in the opposite direction. And instead of barking or gnawing my crate and trying to get at her, I had sympathy for her. Yes, sympathy! A deep heartfelt sympathy for my feline friend in our common plight. We are all alike, I thought. All of us in the animal kingdom are equal victims of "the man." We should unite. "Cats and dogs *could* get along," I shouted to her. "We could be friends. We could live side by side in peaceful harmony, and intermarry and be fruitful and join as one." Clearly I was becoming delusional.

MOOSE-ISM

(REQUEST TO VETERINARIANS) IF IT AIN'T BROKE, DON'T FIX IT.

My crate continued to bump and knock its way along the conveyor belt, until I was finally taken off and driven over to the plane where I was put next to Terrance, an olde (his spelling) English sheepdog, who was also traveling baggage.

Terrance was an older actor, who had been working for years. He was what you might call a journeydog—the kind of actor who has worked his entire life in the business, but never made a name for himself.

After a rather difficult time sussing each other out (it's very hard to sniff someone through a crate), we exchanged pleasantries, and he asked whether I was a working dog, or the lazy kind that just hangs around the house and eats and sleeps. I told him not only was I a working dog, I was an actor too. And this was going to be my last time traveling cargo. He started to laugh. Then he told me a famous joke about actors, which I will share with you.

An east-coast actor had gotten fed up looking for work in

New York, so he was on a train heading west to L.A. At the same time, a west-coast actor was fed up looking for work in L.A., so he was heading east on another train. In Indiana, their trains passed and they each shouted, "Go back, go back, there's no work out there."

I told him that that was very amusing, but it wasn't going to happen to me. I had studied acting. I had already done a commercial. And I already *had* a job. I was flying out to Los Angeles to star in a new television show called *Frasier*.

MOOSE-ISM

THE BEST THINGS IN LIFE ARE WORTH LICKING.

Then Terrance gave me the shock of my young life. He was up for the same role in the same show. The *Frasier* people hadn't sent just for me. I was going to have to audition! And they weren't even sure what they wanted, because Terrance and I were totally different types. My type: handsome, smart, funny, witty, with unlimited talent. His type: homely, slow-witted, not funny, with limited talent.

But Terrance had way more experience than I did. He'd been acting for years and years. Or, as he put it in that froufrou English accent of his, "foa yahs and yahs." And he'd gotten great reviews, copies of which he just happened to have pasted on the inside of his crate. He asked if I would like him to read them to me. "Oh sure," I said, trapped in the cage next to him. It was going to be a lon-n-n-ng trip.

Most of his professional life had been spent acting in regional theater—playing a wide variety of character roles from Crab in *Two Gentleman of Verona* to Sandy in the musical *Annie*, in which Rex Reed said he was riveting.

And he had even tread the boards, as he put it, on the Great White Way: Broadway in New York City. He played the title role in an adaptation of Conan Doyle's *The Hound of the Baskervilles*. Terrance thought the play was going to be his big break. And he's got a real grudge about it, let me tell you. Jabber, jabber, jabber the whole trip. Secretly, I was kind of glad someone had put a pin in this windbag.

His play opened in '86, when *The New York Times* reviewer, Frank Rich, still ruled the theater scene. Frank had panned the play, didn't even mention Terrance, which according to Terrance was a gross oversight, and it closed opening night.

All the other critics liked it. Well, all except John Simon, of course.

John Simon was the theater critic for *New York* magazine. I think he still is. I know actors around the world will breathe a sigh of relief when he goes, for the man leaves no turn unstoned. John Simon hated Terrance's performance. And, as he is wont to do, he continued to harangue Terrance for years after, even mentioning him in reviews of other shows. Saying things like, "Pia Zadora gave a dog of a performance, but not as bad as Terrance the olde (his spelling) English sheepdog in *The Hound of the Baskervilles*."

Like many actors, Terrance swore that if he ever met John Simon in person, he'd bite him.

In 1987, Terrance gave Los Angeles a try. But *Married with Children* had just become a hit and everybody was doing shows about shaggy brown briards. If you weren't a Buck look-alike you couldn't get arrested. He lived on residuals that year.

All of his stories just made me more and more anxious. It was a mean world out there. What was I getting into? Then Terrance told me that this audition for *Frasier* was his last shot at the big time; if he didn't get this one, his agent was going to drop him. He didn't know what he would do if that happened. Probably teach at Juilliard.

But he wasn't worried about it. He had heard the *Frasier* people were looking for someone just like him. This really depressed me. The acting business was tougher than I thought. I had gotten caught up in the glory and the glamour, not realizing that there are a lot of actors out there who never get their chance in the spotlight. Poor Terrance, I thought, I probably shouldn't even audition, I should just let him have the part.

Then I noticed he was glancing at me out of the corner of his eye. And he was smiling slightly. That was when I realized this guy Terrance was trying to psych me out. He had told me these stories to depress me.

I got mad. After all, depression is only anger turned inward (I learned that years later from my shrink) and I wasn't going to let this overly hairy English twit get the best of me.

Okay. Maybe I wasn't the only one auditioning for this *Frasier* show. So what? I had a secret weapon. Me. One look at me, and the producers would *have* to let everyone else go. I was going to be a star, and when I got off that plane, people would be there for me. I would be taxied around, and waited on, and my every whim would be catered to.

Okay. Wrong again. When I got off the plane, there was no fanfare at all. And no fans. As a matter of fact, for the first three days, things were pretty bleak. And I realized those walls around the studios are designed to keep people (and animals) out. I started to think that Terrance's story about the L.A. actor and the New York actor was true. I learned a thing or two about being out of work in Hollywood. And they weren't pretty.

Life was pretty rough. But it toughened me. I paid my dues like everyone else. In a funny way, I'm glad it happened, because it makes me appreciate all the more what I have now. But if you're an aspiring young actor or actress, I don't want you to have to suffer the way I did. So, I'm going to fill you in on a few of the rules of the game before you hop on that plane or train or bus or automobile and head out to the land of dreams.

MOOSE-ISM

BRED FOR RATTING, BORN FOR CATTING.

The Twelve Commandments of Show Business According to Moose

1. Don't quit your day job.

2. Get a day job.

3. Take the money.

4. Never turn your back on a producer, unless it's to lift your hind leg.

5. But never, I repeat never, pee on the stage manager.

6. Always eat free food. And ask for a doggy bag.

7. Never forget what they've done to you, but never show them you remember. That way you can bite them when they least expect it.

8. If you're not on the A-list, make friends with someone who is.

9. Always strive to be artistic, then see number three.

10. Beware of foxtails. They work under your skin and cause great pain.

11. Good work can bring you fame, but it rarely goes the other way.

12. They can't take away your parking space if you don't have a car.

7.
My Audition for the Television Show *Frasier*

So, how did I get the part? The truth depends on who's doing the telling and who's doing the listening. My audition for the television show *Frasier* has become Hollywood legend. Like Lana Turner being discovered sipping a soda pop at a drugstore on the corner of Hollywood and Vine. Or Barbra Streisand auditioning for *I Can Get It For You Wholesale* and putting imaginary chewing gum under the seat of her chair.

One story has me in a knock-down drag-out fight with a bull-terrier and to the victor—me—went the part. Not true.

Another claims that I was part of a huge cattle call. (A cattle call is not an audition for cattle, if that's what you're thinking. It means hundreds and hundreds of unknowns are put in a line and the producers pick out the ones they want to audition.) In my case, I'm supposed to have been standing on a stage like in the movie a *A Chorus Line*, and apparently I pushed my main competition, a sandy-haired mutt named Beachem, into the orchestra pit. Not true.

But by far my favorite is how I poisoned all the other actors in a Machiavellian attempt to take over the entire canine acting profession. Not true, although I considered it.

So what happened? What's the real story behind the legend?

Well, I finally got the call three days after arriving in Los Angeles. I was to go to audition for the creators/executive producers David Angell, Peter Casey, and David Lee. These were the guys who had created the TV show *Wings*, which I loved. Loved, loved, loved, loved, loved. (Actually, I had only seen it once, but I know how to suck up with the best of them.) I was nervous. After having known what it was like being unemployed for three days, I knew what was at stake—nothing less than my entire future.

The morning of the audition, I woke up early. I had not slept much the night before because I was what my mother used to describe as "journey proud"—you know, when you are going on a journey and you can't sleep because you are so excited. Well, I was "audition proud."

So, after I woke up, I started the day with my usual yoga stretches—downward-facing dog, upward-facing dog, a few salutations to the sun, and the obligatory headstand.

Then I did my breathing exercises. I lay on the floor on my back and breathed in and out to a count of ten.

Then I practiced speaking from the diaphragm, until a neighbor banged on the wall and screamed for me to quit barking.

So I decided to quietly run through my acting monologues.

For my serious monologue I was planning to do a speech from *I Never Sang for My Father*. I never knew my father, so it's a play that really spoke to me.

For my comic monologue, I'd decided I wanted to show them that I was not only a physical comedian, but also that I could play the classics. So, although it's not a part I would ever be cast in, I did Sylvius in *As You Like It*. You know the one: "Sweet Phoebe, do not scorn me, do not, Phoebe. Say that you love me not, but say not so in bitterness . . ." etcetera, etcetera, etcetera. When I do that monologue, I enter and do an immediate pratfall. Hilarious.

Having prepared myself physically and mentally, it was time to prepare myself emotionally. The way I did that then is the way I do it now. I psyched myself up. I knew that the producers had been looking to cast this part for some time. They had been through everyone in Los Angeles, and now they were looking at actors from the other side of the country. They wanted it cast. They wanted to get it done. They wanted to stop looking. So, that meant they wanted me to be the right guy for the job. Well, if they wanted me so bad, I wasn't going to disappoint them. I was going to be so ready.

MOOSE-ISM

IF IT'S WORTH CHASING, IT'S WORTH SHAKING TILL IT'S DEAD.

And I was. I was relaxed, I was centered, I was ready to give them my best.

The time came and Gary Gero, owner of Birds and Animals Unlimited, loaded about ten of us in our individual crates on a truck. We drove out to meet the producers at a place called Balboa Park. When we got there, the producers took one look at me and one of them said, "He kinda looks like he could be Martin's dog." And the other one said, "Yep." And they hired me on the spot.

I came. They saw. I got it. Animally, I admired the way they covered their enthusiasm as part of a clever negotiating ploy. But like it or not, they were the first to fall under the spell of what has since become known as "Moose Mania."

That's it. That's the whole story. I hope this will put a stop to a few of the vicious rumors that have been circulating around town about me. I'm not saying who's been doing it, but I could point my paw at a couple of scroungy-looking mutts from another show on a different network that we are beating the tar out of in the ratings game. And to those canines on *Dharma and Greg* I say:

One: I did not sleep with anybody to get the part. And two: They did not cast me just because I matched the color of the set.

8.
A Letter to
My Mom

May 8, 1993

Dear Ma,

I met this girl. Her name is Mathilde. She's French, and she's beautiful, and she's the best acting coach a guy could ever have. I know what you're thinking: What happened to Cathy? Well, all I can say is, Cathy who? From now on it's Mathilde, Mathilde, Mathilde. She's my new mentor. But, I got to tell ya, Ma, it wasn't always this way.

Mathilde and I met in California. I had been flown out to Los Angeles to audition for some big Hollywood producers. Big, right, they flew me out cargo. A runner picked me up at the airport, and my first three days in Los Angeles were just hell. I couldn't get into any restaurants, all the museums were closed to my kind, I was a nobody. Worse than a nobody, I was an out-of-work actor.

But, then my luck changed. I auditioned for this show, Frasier, and I got it! (Yep, you'll be seeing me on TV this fall on Thursday nights at 9:30 after Seinfeld.) And suddenly my life came into focus.

Birds and Animals, my managers, produce the live-action animal shows for Universal Studios. They have a compound and acting studio for us there. The day after I got the part, I was hanging out backstage when this Mathilde person showed up. I thought she was just another dog walker coming to take me on a stroll, but something about her seemed different. Her French perfume and French accent drove me wild. I wanted to spend the rest of my life with her. Oh my God, I thought, she's a witch and she's cast a spell on me.

I shook my head and quickly came back to my senses. Then I burst out of my cage and headed for the first bush I could find. But she followed me, and started making goo-goo noises to me, and then she scratched my neck. And it felt so-o-o-o good. And she was so-o-o-o nice, and her perfume reminded me of the south of France, and I had never even been there. And

MOOSE-ISM

NINE LIVES IS NINE TOO MANY.

I thought, well, if this Mathilde is a witch, then she's a good witch, like Glinda the Good Witch of the North. (Toto was one of my heroes.)

Mathilde drove us out to the beach, where she lives in this great house in Santa Monica. Of course, I made it my own right away. She took me upstairs to show me our room—yes, Ma, Mathilde and I will be sleeping in the same room. But don't worry, I'll get the bed and she'll be sleeping on the floor.

After checking out the upstairs, I went all over the rest of the house and sat in every chair. I rubbed my back on the carpet. Sniffed around trying to ascertain the food situation. I found the trash can, which will be good for a late-night snack. And finally I found the place where Mathilde keeps our food. It's a plastic bin with a top on it. I will figure out how to open that later.

I smelled the scent of other animals around and I wanted them to know I had arrived. So, when Mathilde was out of the room, I lifted my leg on the couch. I know, I know, Ma, you always taught me not to go to the bathroom in the house unless there was a really good reason. Or was it that there's never a good reason to go to the bathroom in the house? Whatever. I finished just in time, so Mathilde didn't catch me.

When I realized that I wasn't Mathilde's only charge, I was bummed. I wanted to be the only one in her life. Me, me, and only me. Doesn't everyone get their own person servant when they come to Hollywood? Mathilde was supposed to be mine.

But then I talked to the other guys and I understood. Many of them had been rejects from previous owners. Mathilde had taken them in when nobody else wanted them. She had even rescued some of them from the pound. They had been on death row, and if it hadn't been for Mathilde, well . . . I don't want to think about it.

After she rescued them, she trained them as actors, and many had already gotten big parts. For instance, Barney and Bogus are brothers who are a combination Saint Bernard–golden retriever mix. Yes, they are half-breeds, not pure like us. But you've always taught me that it takes all kinds to make a world, and how boring life would be if we were all the same, and I believe that.

They were in a movie called Outbreak with Dustin Hoffman, one of my favorite actors and role models. They played a pivotal role in the movie as part of a custody battle between Dustin and his ex-wife. And they were almost too good. I missed most of what Dustin was saying because of the interplay between Barmey and Bogus. It just goes to show you that the old adage is true: there are no small parts, only small actors. Of course, I will always prefer the bigger parts, but still . . . . It also goes to show you that W.C. Fields was right: Never share the stage with kids or animals.

Barney was also in Fluke. *He played Fluke's best friend. And both Barney and Bogus are sons of the dog that played Dreyfus on* Empty Nest, *a show I had seen many times with my people in Florida. This was my first brush with a real show-biz family. They were Hollywood royalty, like the Fondas and the Bridgeses. And I respected their lineage.*

Of course, it's harder for someone like me to break into the business without knowing anyone. I have to get by on sheer talent alone.

There's another mix staying at the house, a sheepdog, named Fred. Fred's like me. He came from nowhere and became a big star. He was in Back to the Future II *and* III, The Firm *with Tom Cruise (Fred was the cute one), and TV shows including* Dear John, Family Matters, *and numerous commercials. He's one of the top dogs in the business, but I don't like him. He's got a huge ego, all he talks about is himself, and he thinks the whole world revolves around him. I know what you're thinking, he sounds just like someone you know—my brother Marlboro. But Marlboro would never pee on my bed like Fred did.*

So anyway, Ma, that's about it. That's my living situation out here in La La Land. Oh, wait, I almost forgot to tell you about Mathilde. After a couple of days at her house, I could tell that she liked me more than the others. But I had to test that, because . . . well, you know me.

One morning shortly after I'd arrived, Mathilde gave me a bath and put me outside to dry in the sun. I noticed that one of the boards on the fence was loose. So, of course, I decided to dig under it and escape to see how much Mathilde cared about me.

Well, she passed with flying colors, 'cause she went nuts with worry. She put flyers out, she called all her friends to help, and she got in her car and went driving all over the neighborhood. At least, that's what she told me later.

While she was doing that, I was having the time of my life. I fought a dog. A smaller dog than me, which I prefer. I chased an opossum, ate some garbage, rolled in dog poop to get that awful bath smell off me. Then I almost got hit by a car on Main Street. Yeah. That surprised you, didn't it? It surprised me too. The car slammed on its brakes and I was inches from the bumper.

It also surprised the couple that almost hit me. So much so that they took me to the vet to make sure I was all right. I was fine, but because of the dog poop, the vet started giving me another bath. I didn't have my identification tags on, and they didn't realize who I was, so the couple was planning to keep me.

In the middle of my bath, Mathilde came in. She just got lucky and found me—call it kismet. When she saw me there she burst into tears. Then the people burst into tears. And the vet burst into tears. And I burst into tears because the vet wasn't paying attention and I got suds in my eyes.

Anyway, after Mathilde explained who I was, the people naturally wanted ransom money. But Mathilde managed to convince them that my autograph was worth way more than any ransom. Which is, of course, true.

The vet finished bathing me, and Mathilde took me home and gave me a good scolding. She was really upset because something might have happened to her number-one star. See, she recognizes in me her chance to climb out of obscurity. She hopes to go from being just another animal trainer/acting teacher to being an animal trainer/acting teacher to a star. She might even become famous too, and be able to get a table at Spago between seven and ten.

Mathilde often says that she can pick a talented dog out of any crowd right away. And she's picked me as her favorite. With Mathilde at my side, I know that I can be one of the great actors of all time.

So, Ma, you can see how lucky I am. Mathilde takes really good care of me. She is always on the lookout, making sure that I only get the best of whatever it is I need. And although she'll never take the place of you in my heart, Mathilde is the new woman in my life. I hope that's okay with you. Give my best to Dad if you see him.

Love,
Moosie

P.S. Don't ever *tell* anyone I let you call me that.

9.
She Said,
He Said

Mathilde

The first thing to remember is that dogs have personalities too, just like we do.

Moose

The first thing to remember is that people have personalities too, just like we do.

Mathilde

Try to pick the ones who say "me, me, me!" with their excited eyes and tails wagging. They're usually the best.

Moose

Try to pick the ones who drive Mercedes. They're usually the best.

Mathilde

When I first started working with
Moose, I soon realized that he was
going to be a handful. He's a very
complex little dog because:
a) he is a Jack Russell Terrier,
b) he is Moose, and
c) he has an attitude.

Moose

When I first started working
with Mathilde, I soon realized
that she was going to be difficult.
Mathilde is a very complex
person because:
a) she is a woman,
b) she is French, and
c) she is a French woman.

Mathilde

Moose was much pushier than
any *dog* I had ever seen. He
always wanted to be in charge
(still does). Everything had to be his way.

Moose

Mathilde was much pushier than
any *person* I had ever seen,
and most barnyard animals.
She always wanted to be in charge
(still does). Everything
had to be her way.

Mathilde

Moose has to have been the
most difficult dog I ever trained.
He acted like he'd been taught
nothing, and I knew that was not
true. He was independent, selfish,
challenging, demanding, feisty,
impatient, intense, arrogant,
stubborn, but above all he was
strong-willed. Everything I tried to
get him to do, from sitting to
heeling to barking on cue was
a battle of wills between us.

Moose

So?

Mathilde

He even chewed up my prize bougainvillea.

Moose

It was my way of telling her
it didn't look right in that spot.

Mathilde

When I first got Moose, he was
not a sweet, loving little dog.
He wasn't demonstrative or
friendly with people. He was
much too independent for that.
He never wanted to be petted and
didn't want to be hugged.
So I started to massage him.

Moose

When I first hooked up
with Mathilde,
she always wanted to pet me.
I used to hate that. So I made
her massage me.

Mathilde

I spent hours and hours giving
him deep tissue massages that
he enjoyed very much.

Moose

Mmmmmmmmmmm.

Mathilde

Every time that I would touch
him I would only massage him.

Moose

Oh, baby.

Mathilde

I did this for a very long time,
and eventually he would move
his body toward me when he
felt like having a good rub and
pretty soon he really turned out
to be much more cuddly, and that
help him improve his social skills.

Moose

Whatever you say, dear.

Mathilde

Now he follows me everywhere
and does pretty much whatever I say.
It was because of that I won
the battle of wills.

Moose

Uh-uh. Who's getting massaged every day?

Mathilde

It would take a whole book to
tell you how I trained this
difficult dog, but he's been worth it.

Moose

I'm still training Mathilde.
But she's worth it. I may
even write a book about it.

Mathilde

Different techniques work for
different dogs. Keep at it and you
will find a way. And remember:
if a dog is well trained, you can
take him anywhere. He will
become a loyal and loving companion
for life.

Moose

Different techniques work for
different people. Keep at it and you
will find a way. And remember:
If a person is well trained,
you can take her anywhere.
She will become a loyal and
loving companion for life.

10.
The *Frasier* Chronicles

My week starts on a Thursday. That's because *Frasier* tapes—sorry, films (some people get so upset when you say a filmed show is taped)—*Frasier* films on Tuesday nights.

So, on Wednesday mornings the cast is presented with a new script. This is often the first time the actors get to see their new parts, so they usually spend the first part of the morning seeing which scenes they are in and counting how many lines they have.

Once that's done, the cast and writers, producers, and various hangers-on sit around a table, drink coffee, and eat bagels while the actors read the script out loud. I'm not there for that. I let the stage manager read my part.

Afterwards, the actors go home for the day, while the writers rewrite the script based on what did and didn't work at the reading. This almost inevitably leads to a bigger part for me. When something's not working, you bring in your heavy hitter.

The next morning, Thursday, is my first day of rehearsal. And since the other actors need more help than I do, they call in a special person called a "director" to help them. They rehearse their scenes with the director, while I go over my crucial moments with Mathilde.

I know what you're thinking. I'm so natural that it seems like I'm making it up each week. But my action in a scene is never impromptu. If I started goofing around it would throw the other actors off. They're not as good as I am at improvisation.

Normally, I could rehearse in two days. I already know most of the behaviors I need for the show—retrieving, raising a paw, or burying my head under a pillow. But I go to the set four days a week for a couple of hours each day, because the writers and actors like to rehearse with me. I'm a team player and I'm always willing to help the others find their way.

MOOSE-ISM

SOMETIMES THERE'S NOTHING BETTER THAN CHASING YOUR OWN TAIL.

When Mathilde and I first approach a scene, she walks me around the set, talking about the scene and my action in it. Then we figure out what my character, Eddie, wants and needs, and what are the obstacles to him getting what he wants and needs. Then all we have to do is decide how he's going to overcome those obstacles. It's all basic Acting 101 stuff.

For instance, in one episode, Eddie wanted a piece of Frasier's muffin, but Frasier didn't want to give it to him. I considered the various ways Eddie could get the muffin. First, I thought Eddie could try staring. (I'll talk about "the stare" in a later chapter.) But that didn't work; Frasier just put his paper up in front of him (an obstacle). So I considered having Eddie grab his pants leg, or hop on a chair, but then I decided simply to have Eddie jump up and down (remember the kangaroo jump?), rising up over his paper and catching Frasier's eye. This worked. Eddie achieved his goal and got a piece of muffin, which we both got to eat. It's one of the things I love most about acting.

In the past, Eddie's parts have been relatively simple. He has gotten his head stuck in a tub of ice cream. Had to sneeze on cue. Run across the apartment with a pack of cigarettes in his mouth. Come running when he heard the word "walk," and run for cover when he heard the word "bath." He drank from the toilet. (Disgusting.) And he's paraded around the apartment with Daphne's bra in his mouth. (Neato.)

But no matter how simple the action or, as they say in the biz, piece of business, the creative part for me is always in the how. How am I going to execute any particular piece of business? And I base the how on Eddie's relationships with the other characters on the show. Not *my* relationship with the other actors; you all know from the first chapter that we adore each other, but how does the character Eddie relate to the others? How does he feel about Niles, Martin, Daphne, Roz, and of course Frasier?

Let's start with America's favorite character, and, coincidentally, my favorite as well—Eddie.

I think it helps to first understand the differences between me and Eddie. Yes, we both are very special dogs that come from a loving and supportive family. But Eddie has only lived with Martin, whereas you know that I have shuffled around a bit in my life.

Also, I'm much feistier than Eddie is. He's more content to sit around the house and do nothing, while I'm always on the go. I prefer working to sitting around at home, which bores me. I'm a hyper dog. You need to keep me busy or I'll destroy your house in a hurry.

We both demand our morning and our afternoon walk in the park where we can go crazy and run around and hit all the trees. We like chasing squirrels and, well, that we are both fatally attracted to cats is a given. We also like to explore holes and roll around in garbage.

We hate baths and having our teeth brushed. But we both like to bang on the cupboard doors and work them open with our nose. And we agree that anything we can do to dig or chew or be obnoxious is good. Eddie is extremely bright and smart and knows just about everything, as do I.

But Eddie has a specific past and a specific point of view, different from mine. And although the writers haven't told me too much about his past, I have done what all good actors do and created a "bible" or "back-story" for my character. The *Frasier* writers may have a different one, but who cares? I'm playing the part.

My thinking is that shortly after his wife died, Martin got young Eddie to keep him company. They became best friends right away. Frasier and Niles were both jealous of him, like a parent bringing a new kid into the house. But they got over it because Eddie brought so much joy into Martin's life. Eddie and Martin were inseparable, doing everything together. Martin even let Eddie go on patrols in the police car—strictly against policy.

But all the fun came slamming to a halt when Martin got shot in the hip and they had to go live with Frasier. Eddie didn't like it any more than Martin did. All the old comforts of home were gone. His favorite couch, the rug he'd torn the end fringe off of, all the old wooden spoons he'd chewed on. But Eddie did find one good benefit from the move: there were ever increasing ways he could annoy Frasier.

One day, he noticed Frasier had a piece of cracker on his cheek.

Eddie started staring at the cracker, hoping that it would fall off said cheek and he could eat it. Frasier thought Eddie was staring at him, and when Eddie realized how much this annoyed Frasier, he started doing it on purpose. Thus "the stare" was born.

I like to keep the stare fresh, so I make up different reasons to do it each time they put it in the script. Sometimes Eddie just wants Frasier to know that he likes him, other times he's trying to get Frasier to give him some food, and still other times he's just bored and looking for something fun to do, and he decides, what could be more fun than to annoy Frasier?

Niles? Well, Eddie enjoys annoying Niles too. Eddie is blue-collar—like Martin—and he doesn't understand the Crane boys' high-falutin ways. But he does have a special connection to Niles because he was the first one in the house to realize that Niles was in love with Daphne. He sensed it because Eddie feels the same way about Maris. Yes, Maris. He loves her because she reminds him of a big bone.

He likes Roz a lot, though he doesn't get to see her enough. I think that's a relationship that hasn't been explored thoroughly enough on the show. Maybe Eddie and Roz could have a spin-off together? (To the *Frasier* writers, if you're reading this: hint, hint.) Like everyone else, Eddie thinks of Roz as a good-time girl. He hopes one day he'll get to nuzzle in that ample bosom of hers.

Daphne is someone Eddie could take home to his mother. He adores her; and not just because she takes care of him, and feeds him, and takes him on long walks, but because she's kind and considerate and smells good. By the way, it's not shampoo that makes her smell so good. It's *********. (That was edited by the Paramount censors. They don't want the secret to get out.) Eddie loves Daphne's accent.

And if it weren't for that ridiculous six-month quarantine period, he'd like to visit England with her.

Needless to say, Eddie would do anything for Martin. John Mahoney said it and it's true: "Eddie is a one-person dog." He worships the ground Martin walks on. And while a Jack Russell terrier is always going to be a little independent, if there is one person in his life that Eddie would give up that independence for, it would be Martin.

So, keeping all these complicated relationships in mind, I make my choices and then work my part in with the other actors. On Thursday afternoon, we do a run-through for the writers/producers. After that, we go home, and the writers once again rewrite what doesn't work in the script. And once again, it usually leads to me having an even bigger part.

On Friday, it's just more of the same. We rehearse any changes that the writers have made in the script, then we have another run-through and the writers rewrite again.

Weekends we have off. Run on the beach. Chase squirrels. Work on my tan, then back to work on Monday.

Camera-blocking day. That's when we run through the blocking for the camera crew and they set up their shots. This is a good day for the other actors, because they get to set all their movements, and make sure that they have my cues right. Mathilde says that the hardest part for me is to learn new patterns each week, but by Monday, it's child's play. Which is why, most of the time, they use a stuffed dog as my stand-in.

Tuesday is show day. And although I'm covered with hair, and I walk on all fours, and I usually never know what time it is or what day it is, because I never learned to read a calendar or to tell time, and I never graduated high school, much less college, I always know when it's show day at *Frasier*.

Animal instinct? Maybe. That's what Mathilde thinks. But what people attribute to instinct in us is usually just common sense. You *think* it's animal instinct because you don't *think* we *think*. But, I mean come on. How dumb would I have to be? I always get a special bath on show day, and a spray of Holiday cologne for dogs. Why? Because people like to come up and pet me and kiss me. And these people have been standing in the hot sun all day waiting to get into a taping of *Frasier*, and they smell. So, Mathilde squirts me with cologne so I can stand it.

One of my favorite parts is when Mathilde and I do our preshow act for the audience. We make our entrance to thunderous applause. Then we answer questions and perform special tricks for the audience. It's shameless pandering to the groundlings, but it works. They love me.

MOOSE-ISM

IF YOU GOT 'EM, LICK 'EM.

Then I go backstage to prepare. I can hear the audience rustling in their seats and I start bubbling with excitement. My ears perk up, and I become hyper-alert. A bell rings. The first A.D. yells, "Quiet." And the director calls, "Action." And the filming begins. It's everything I can do to wait for my cue, I'm always so eager to get on stage and do my part.

And I'm brilliant. Always. Okay, not always. Once in a while, because of all the exhausting work, I do, like John said, short-circuit and forget things.

One particular night, I was supposed to run across the stage and find a pair of socks under Frasier's couch. I started out and got halfway there, and couldn't remember what to do, so I stopped, and then I remembered I was supposed to roll over, so I started doing that, but then I remembered that wasn't it, I was supposed to get the remote, so I got the remote in my mouth and thought, wait a minute, that's not it either, so then I just decided to play dead. The audience howled (I always know how to get my laugh), but it was wrong for the scene.

I had lost my motivation because I had forgotten what the scene was about. Mathilde was forced to run across the stage, out of camera range, to remind me.

They say four-camera shows are the most difficult for dogs and their trainers, because you have to know where to be at all times, and where the cameras are. So I screw up occasionally. So what?

Even executive producer Christopher Lloyd admits I'm "a pretty quick study." The only problem he sees is that "now all the actors are expecting to be tossed dog treats when they hit their marks."

After the show is over, I am always the first one out to take my bow. And guess who gets the longest ovation? Kelsey? Jane? David? John? Peri? Well, I'm not saying. Come to a filming and see for yourself.

But the winner was . . .

Over the last six years, I've given some terrific performances. They've all been good, of course, but some have been really extraordinary. And yet I have never won an Emmy, or even been nominated for one, because the Academy of Television Arts and Sciences has never recognized what animal actors contribute to the art and science of television.

Well, let me ask you, reader, what do you think?

It was the beginning of the 1993–94 season. In the pilot episode, Frasier had just moved to Seattle where he was starting a new life as a talk-radio psychiatrist. His life took a surprising turn when his father, his father's dog (me), and a slightly psychic health-care specialist moved in with him. In the final, pivotal moment of the show, Eddie the dog (again moi) jumped up on the couch and stared at Frasier. The stare would become one of the signature events of the television age: like Carol Burnett tugging on her ear, Milton Berle wearing a dress, or Lucy saying, "Ethel, I've got a plan." **But the winner was . . . Kelsey Grammer** for Best Actor in a Comedy.

Okay. I understood him winning that year; after all, he had been practically an unknown on that show *Cheers* for all those years, so it was a pity vote. I could give him that one.

But the winner was . . . Kelsey Grammer again in the 1994–95 season. What's that you say? Even after your brave and heart-breaking performance in "The Unkindest Cut of All"? Yes. Even after I literally gave the best part of me, they gave the award to him.

Now it's 1995–1996. Surely, that was going to be the year of the Moose. Did they notice your performance in "Leapin' Lizards"? The way you showed America "thunder-fear" by hiding under pillows? Noooooooooo. They should have, **but the winner was . . . John Lithgow,** that wacky alien from *Third Rock from the Sun*.

Okay, okay. He was a movie star who deigned to do television. The Academy have always been snobs about that sort of thing. He gets his Emmy, I'm fine with that. So, in 1996–97, after I gave the vivid portrayal of a dog depressed in "Death and the Dog" (a performance which was stolen outright by Nicolas Cage in *Leaving Las*

Vegas), I figured it was my turn, **but the winner was . . . John Lithgow** again. Hah! Will the injustice never end?

Not in the 1997–1998 season. Not even after I showed America *Lilith-fear* in the "Room Service" episode. Did the Academy see fit to give it to me? You would think. **But the winner was . . . Kelsey Grammer.**

And this year? Well, someone didn't even get a nomination! Not after I drove Niles crazy in "Dial M for Martin" or after I wore the Santa suit in "Merry Christmas, Mrs. Merkowitz." Not a nod. Not a mention. Nothing. It should have been me, **but the winner was. . . John Lithgow.**

I don't care. I'm sick of the whole damn mess. I'm just going to keep doing good work, and be satisfied with the knowledge that I'm loved by millions of adoring fans around the world. But if I ever have to play a depressed dog again, I won't have to act.

11.
The Stare

So what about it? The famous stare. The stare that's made *Frasier* a top-ten show. It certainly deserves its own chapter.

Originally, they were looking for a dog that would bother Frasier. But not just any dog. One that took an immediate liking to him—a small, hyper, annoying one that stared at him all the time. The idea was that it would drive a guy like Frasier nuts.

Well, the last thing Jack Russell terriers do is stare. We bounce off the walls, we tear up furniture, we plan delicious kitty menus. But, since the part called for a stare, I had to figure out a way to do it.

But how? How? I couldn't figure out how. And then Mathilde came up with a great idea. She showed me an old tape of *The Jack Benny Show*. And suddenly I found my inspiration. Jack Benny was the master of the deadpan stare. So I just copied him.

Yeah. It's true. I copied Jack Benny. But we look so different no one has ever realized it. Until now, that is. And I don't mind admitting it because I feel that although I got the idea from him, I've definitely put my own spin on it.

I brought it in to rehearsal that first week, and the producers loved it. We put it in the pilot episode exactly as I had developed it. And voila! Television history.

As a matter of fact, for the first year the role of Eddie was "the stare." And it became so important in Eddie's relationship with Frasier that in one episode they had Frasier get even by staring down Eddie. It was amusing to watch Kelsey attempt to do what I do.

My stare was funny, but I couldn't milk that forever. And there was an uprising across America, because people wanted to see me do more. You got to give the people what the people want. So the producers started putting in other things for me to do. I, of course, rose to the occasion. And, voila! More history.

But my main role in the show is the little irritant that will never go away. When the writers deviate too much from my mission, I have to remind them of what I'm all about, so I politely suggest that they have me stare Frasier down again. They must always remember that I am the Jack Benny of the show and Frasier is my Rochester.

12.
Player
Pooch

Well, whether I'm an Emmy winner or not doesn't really matter, because ever since *Frasier* came on the air, I've been a star. Star, star, star, star, star. And I got to tell you, life is pretty darn good. Although, it's not all limousines and bikini-clad women throwing themselves at you, you know.

Okay, it is. It's that and more. It's great. It's incredible. It's unbelievable. Everybody should be one.

Okay, maybe that's going a little too far. Because if everyone was a star, we stars wouldn't have anyone to lord it over. But you shouldn't be jealous just because we get to hang out with all the best people, and go to all the best places, and have our every whim catered to. Stars have problems, too.

For instance, you're going to an opening in your limousine, and there is a long line of cars in front of you. And your limousine driver lets you out a full half block away from the entrance to the theater. Well, you've got to walk the rest of the way—by yourself!

Or you order a bracelet for your girlfriend at Harry Winston's, but they give you the wrong size diamond and you have to send it back.

Plus, at Christmastime you have to tip everyone. Your house-keeper, and your gardener, and your pool man, and your limo driver, and your groomer, and your pedicurist, and your masseuse, and your flea dipper—you're like Santa Claus to the world. Sometimes I long for the old days when I was just a nobody. Okay, I'm lying.

It's great, baby, great. All of it. But I was exaggerating before; I don't really have a pedicurist—my groomer does my nails. But I do have an agent, publicist, body double, and a long-term contract with the studio. In the last few years, I've done things that only kings would dream of. I've stayed at some incredible hotels—the Ritz-Carlton in Chicago and Cleveland, the Essex House in New York City, the Four Seasons in Seattle. And eaten at some fabulous restaurants—the Polo Lounge at the Beverly Hills Hotel, La Bernadin in New York, and Roscoe's Chicken and Waffles in Los Angeles.

MOOSE-ISM

FRENCH WOMEN ARE THE BEST. AND I'M NOT JUST SAYING THAT TO GET A TREAT.

And now that I'm a star, Hollywood has opened its doors to me. I'm on the A-list now, baby. You *want* to be seen with me. Take a look at the glossy photos in the center.

Not bad, huh? But that's not the half of it. Get a load of this.

January 18, 1995

Ms. Mathilde De Cagny
Paramount Television
Frasier Show—Stage 25
5555 Melrose Avenue
Los Angeles, CA 90038

Dear Mathilde,

On behalf of Frito-Lay, I'd like to formally invite you and a guest to join us at Super Bowl XXIX in Florida later this month. We're planning a special Advertising Premiere on Saturday night (January 28) for our key VIP retail customers and are creating a walk-on personal appearance for you in conjunction with screening your ad. We'll also provide two tickets for you to Sunday's game!

A suite has already been reserved in your name for Saturday and Sunday nights. In addition to two first-class, round-trip airfares, we'll also provide your transportation while in Florida—including airport pick-up, travel to Saturday's rehearsal and event, to the game on Sunday, and return to the airport.

Please don't hesitate to call with any questions regarding these details. I look forward to seeing you later this month.

Sincerely,
Tod J. MacKenzie
Vice President,
Advertising & Public Affairs

Yeah. That's right. The Super Bowl! Jealous, aren't you? I was thrilled. I didn't know much about football, except that they played with a ball made from a pig. Anytime I can see pigs fly, I'm there.

And I saw the ticket—first class on American Airlines—no more steerage for me! I always fly American now. The other airlines won't allow dogs in the cabin, not even celebrated ones like me. But good old American allows a select few to fly, and I'm one of them.

Unlike my first trip, when I was dragged through the airport on a leash, this time there was someone from special services to meet us as we were getting out of the limo. Sean was a very nice guy with an Australian accent. He looked after us and made sure that our (my) every need was taken care of. And I got to ride in the V.I.D. (Very Important Dogs) golf cart.

As I was boarding, the pilot announced I was on the plane. So much for traveling incognito. But it did mean I got to go into the cockpit and look at all the instruments. Wow, it was like being on the *Star Trek* set. And I gotta say, if I ever worried about flying before, no longer. I swear that plane looked like it could fly itself.

They didn't let me take off in the cockpit with them because of "regulations" (I think you can do it in Canada), so I went back to my first class seat to get ready for takeoff. I always get the window seat, even though I know Mathilde likes it. When Mathilde and I have a conflict, it's always a hard decision for me. I mean after all, she has taught me almost everything I know. But I support her now, so I get the window.

She puts my special blanket on the seat, and I'm served caviar and champagne with the best of them. And folks love it when I'm on the plane. Except for this one woman who was allergic to dogs and so she had to be removed. I'm always signing autographs, and getting my picture taken to the point where I'm exhausted. I've tried disguising myself—wearing sunglasses and curling my hair like a poodle—but people still recognize me. So I remind myself that without those fans, I'm just another terrier, and it could be back to steerage for me.

Even with all the hoopla about my being on board, would you believe that I had to prove to this fat guy sitting behind me that I was really me by doing some of my famous tricks? Some people shouldn't drink on airplanes.

Then the guy became like my best friend in the world, and I thought, oh, boy, it's going to be one of those trips. I'm sure it's happened to you. When the person sitting near you on a plane is a talker and all you really want is to be left alone? At least this guy wasn't trying to psych me out of an audition like Terrance, the olde English sheepdog.

Of course, the guy was so drunk that he fell asleep before we even took off, and slept the entire trip. This actually worked out well for me, because I had really bad gas that trip and was able to blame it on him. And it was lucky for Mathilde too, because I usually blame it on her.

I hate to say this, because you're going to think it's so cliché, but my absolute favorite time on an airplane is when food is being served. They bring me my very own tray and everything.

But I've had to learn to wait patiently for my turn. I've also learned that if you sit up front in the airplane you get served first. And if you sit in the back, even in first class, they are usually out of your choice of entrée by the time they get to you. Plus, the seat in the back row won't recline all the way back. It's, if you'll excuse the expression, a major pet peeve of mine. I can't believe they let airlines get away with that.

After lunch, I had a delicious nap, and woke up just in time for landing. Naturally, there was a limo waiting for us. There always is. And it's limos only, please. Only on rare occasions will I allow myself to travel in a town car.

We arrived at the Marriott Hotel, where we were given a luxurious suite. And there was a huge basket waiting for me, with all kinds of treats. (Mathilde got a little one.) The hotel had even made me my own robe.

We went from party to party, and saw a fantastic game. I had to have my picture taken with what felt like everyone in Florida, but you know what they say, there are no free rides.

The flight home was more of the same, although this time I had the chicken—if I don't watch my figure, no one will. And when the flight attendants gave out the newspapers I noticed that *USA Today* had a front-page article on me. That was nice.

I arrived home, tired but content. I love to travel. Car or plane, it's one of my favorite things to do. I have a Mileage Plus card under Mr. Eddie Frasier. And those frequent-flyer miles are really piling up.

13.
My Incredible Range

According to the television industry, a dog is worth two points in prime time. One point represents 850,000 TV sets. So that means that on *Frasier*, I alone am responsible for bringing in 1.7 million viewers. Needless to say, that puts me in constant demand for other jobs and acting gigs besides *Frasier*.

Personal Appearances

Twice, Paramount has taken me to Las Vegas for the annual convention of television owners and managers. I sit and pose with them, and have my picture taken and bark on cue—all in order to get them to buy *Frasier* for syndication. And it worked, because we are all over the place. I did this because every time *Frasier* plays on television, I get a million dollars.

Yeah. Right.

Commercials

I did a commercial for fat-free pretzels with Jason Alexander. It was a Rold Gold Pretzel commercial, and Jason was absolutely wonderful to work with. First he chased me through the airport and then we ended up jumping out of a plane together. He's a consummate professional, and I'm not just saying that because I was strapped to him for dear life as we were hurled from an airplane, or because he fed me pretzels between takes.

No, it was one of those chemistry things, really. He was right there for me when I needed him, and I tried to be there for him in his big moments. I'd love to do my next picture with him. I think he'd be a hoot.

Lloyd Bridges was in the commercial, too, but he was playing the bad guy, and since I'm a method actor, I didn't talk to him for fear that it would mess up my concentration.

I've also done a couple of Kentucky Fried Chicken spots during the last couple of Super Bowls. They went well too, but I thought I'd get to eat more of the chicken.

Print Work

In 1995, I did my own Eddie "beefcake" calendar. Yeah, people were begging for it, so I obliged. And I didn't mind doing a few suggestive poses, but I drew the line at flat-out nudity. I believe in leaving something to the imagination. Somebody has to set the moral standards in this country.

In 1998, they put me on the cover of the Coach Christmas catalog and they sold out three weeks before Christmas. I didn't have to lift a finger, just show my *punem*. (*Punem* is the Jewish word for face. I'm bilingual.)

Magazine Covers

I've been on so many magazine covers I lose track sometimes, but as far as I can recall they've included:

- *L.A. TV Times* cover—December 19–25, 1993.

- *Entertainment Weekly*—December 1993. I was on the cover, plus there was an article about me. It's worth trying to find an old copy because it makes a really good read.

• *TV Guide* cover—June 18, 1994 (alone). In the same issue, I got a thumbs up. And I quote: "The Paws That Refresh. A big wet doggy kiss to *Frasier's* secret weapon: Eddie, a clever little canine who walks off with the show each week with his patented pesky-pooch pose. The hound has stolen our hearts."

• *Life* Magazine (with Kelsey)—October 1994.

• *US* Magazine—January 1995 (cover w/ Tom Hanks, Keanu Reeves, Helen Hunt, Tom Cruise, etc.). Only the hottest stars in Hollywood that year.

• *TV Guide* cover—October 3, 1998 (but with the cast this time). They wanted to use just me again, but I insisted they put the rest of the cast on the cover with me. They were getting jealous, and I didn't want any hard feelings on the set.

MOOSE-ISM

THUMBS ARE OVERRATED.

Movies

I'll be honest. I haven't done as much movie work as I would like. I know. Every television star wants to be a movie star. Or at least direct. Well, you know what? I like my job. I like performing in front of a live audience. And I like going into millions of homes each week and making people laugh.

That said, I was in *My Dog Skip* with Kevin Bacon. The lead role was originally offered to me, but I thought I was too old for it, so I had them give it to my son Enzo. I played Skip in his older years, which I filled with my usual pathos. I made women cry. I'll probably get an Oscar. And, yeah, that means in the Kevin Bacon game, I'm first degree.

I've also done some music videos with Stone Temple Pilots, and Clint Black. Music videos are *like* movies, aren't they?

Charity Work

No matter how full my busy schedule, I have always found time to help raise money for a good cause. I've participated in a host of charity events, including:

- Paws/LA: They provide dog care for people with AIDS.

- Actors and Others for Animals, which promotes the humane treatment of animals.

- The Entertainment Industry Foundation Women's Cancer Research Alliance.

- Wagathon, a four kilometer-walk for animals led by none other than yours truly.

- Kennel Kapers, a shelter for homeless animals.

In addition, I had my paw prints embedded in concrete as part of Purina's Pawprint Wall of Fame to raise money for the Pets for People Program, a pet shelter and animal adoption program which is helping to deal with the problem of pet overpopulation. My paw prints are on permanent display at the Los Angeles Society for the Prevention of Cruelty to Animals. It's the animal equivalent of having your footprints at Grauman's Chinese Theatre.

All totaled, I have helped raise over twenty-five thousand dollars for various causes. What can I say? Saint Moose, perhaps?

14.
My Private Life

I don't like to talk about my private life. And I don't believe just because I'm a celebrity I owe the public every personal detail of my life. However, like most celebrities, I have kept a diary, which I intend to have published posthumously. The following is an excerpt from that diary about my first time with a woman. Everybody's first time is special, and mine was no exception.

March 7, 1993
My First Love

She was over there. I could smell her. It was either her or the lilac bush; either way, she smelled good. She was in the room two fences down from mine. I knew that because I saw Mathilde putting her there. It happened about two days ago. I was chasing a squirrel. Because I liked chasing it and well . . . that's what we do. Dogs chase things. And when we catch them, we shake them with our teeth. I know. It's crude and a little bohemian, but it's a dog-eat-squirrel world out there.

Anyway, I was chasing the squirrel, and lying in the shade, and chas-

ing, and lying and chasing and lying, stopping for the occasional drink of water, when I heard everyone going crazy. All the other guys were barking and jumping up and down, especially the little Pekingese who does commercials for sausages while sitting in the fat lady's pocketbook.

With all that commotion going on, I was naturally curious, so I peeked through the hole in the fence (a hole, by the way, which I had gnawed through the wood for this very purpose). Through it, I could see into Mathilde's house. And there I saw a vision in fur. Loveliness personified in the form of a puppy. Actually, she looked a lot like me, only she had curves where I didn't, and perky little ears you could nibble on for hours. I was more than a little excited, especially when Mathilde brought her outside and told me that this cute little ball of fur's name was Folie, which means crazy in French, and which also meant that I was crazy for her. Me! Me! Oh, my god, me! Just the thought of her and me together made chasing the squirrel seem positively mundane. If the truth be known, I was still a virgin at the time. It's not something I'm proud of, but true nonetheless. When I first saw Folie, well . . . I wanted her and I wanted her bad. The only problem was, how was I going to get her?

MOOSE-ISM

TO BARK OR NOT TO BARK, THAT IS THE QUESTION.

Mathilde had built houses for all my friends (and enemies) in her backyard. Each of us had our own room, and plenty of toys, food, and drink. Some might think we were spoiled, but I didn't see it that way. I saw it as my destiny. As that fellow Shakespeare wrote (Mathilde took me to see Shakespeare in Love): "Some are born great, some achieve greatness and some have greatness thrust upon them." I don't know which one of those applies to me, I just know I'm pretty great.

Before Stardom

After
Stardom

Anyway, as I was saying, we each have our own rooms, and Folie—beautiful Folie. Yummy, sexy Folie. Folie with the red collar on. . . . Where was I? Oh, yes, Folie was being housed two rooms away from mine. Why she wasn't in the room right next to mine is a testament to how well Mathilde knows me. I've dug under, ripped apart, and jumped over more fences in my lifetime than Purina makes kibble. And I wasn't going to let a few fences get in between me and Miss Heaven on Earth over there.

MOOSE-ISM

CARPE KITTY (SEIZE THE CAT).

She wanted me too I could tell. When she first arrived, she caught me looking at her through the fence, and she gave me such a come-hither look, that I almost came hither right then and there. Then she arched her back and turned away from me—like she didn't care. Oh, she cared all right. She cared enough to howl like a crazy woman every time they left her alone. She was howling for a little co-Eddie company, if you know what I mean. I just had to get over there.

It was the morning of my first day of work on this new television show called Frasier. Mathilde was all nervous and everything. She had even given me a bath the night before—I hate baths. She seemed to think there was a lot riding on this day. I don't know what her problem was. All I had to do was stare at this guy. I mean, how hard was that? But she seemed to think it was very important. Way more important than, say, enjoying happy hour with the babe two rooms over.

I was waiting for Mathilde to take me to work, when the squirrel ran so close to me that I had no choice but to try to grab her tail with my teeth. Just as I was about to catch her, she hopped up the tree and turned around and laughed at me.

Now this tree I'm talking about was an old California live oak—all gnarly and twisted and stretched out over the whole backyard, and. . . . Stretched out over the whole backyard! *Bingo! How hard could it be to climb a tree? I mean if the squirrel could do it. . . ?*

I could see it was getting to be time to go. Mathilde was getting our stuff together. Really her stuff—you know women and the way they pack. She was putting my special water bowl in her bag, along with my comb, and brush, and a few of my favorite toys. She put in another bag filled with treats. Wait a minute, treats? No, Folie was a bigger treat, she was a treat-ess. When Mathilde picked up my leash and headed for the door, I knew she meant to take me to work.

Suddenly, I started thinking, "If I leave this place, Folie might not be here when I get back. Or she might find another boyfriend. That French poodle was checking Folie out, along with everyone else in the yard. Give that Frenchy half a chance and, well, you know how the French are in matters of the heart. What if Folie fell for another guy?"

Just as Mathilde started to open the door, the telephone rang. She went to answer it and I decided I had to do something and do something quick.

I got as far away from the trunk of the tree as I could. The squirrel just sat there and smirked at me. She thought I was still trying to get her. That's the thing about squirrels, they always think everything is about them. From the corner of my room, I started running at the tree and then I took a flying leap right onto the branch next to the squirrel. That sure as hell wiped the smile off her whiskers.

She shot up about three feet into the air and went sailing smack on top of the rottweiler below. As funny as that was, I didn't have time to laugh.

Mathilde was bound to come for me soon, and I had a date with destiny. Actually, a date with Folie. Destiny is the Chihuahua with the really bad breath who lives next door.

I walked along the limb, over two rooms and there she was, lying on the grass next to her water bowl, looking just as fetching as ever. She looked up at me, surprised no doubt to see me looking down at her. Then she looked away—like it was an everyday occurrence and she wasn't even interested! For a second there, I felt like a fool. I had climbed a tree to get to my honey, and all she was giving me

MOOSE-ISM

TO ERR IS HUMAN, TO FORGIVE CA-NINE.

was attitude. Fortunately for both of us, she glanced up again with a sly but eager expression on her face, and she raised her tail a little bit. I realized she wasn't being aloof, she was just shy!

Well, shyness I could get around. I hurled myself from the tree branch onto her roof, and then I hopped down next to her and started sniffing her butt, you know, the way we dogs do. I don't know what we're sniffing for, but my father did it, his father did it and his father before him—you don't mess with tradition.

And there it was again. That smell. It was her or the lilacs, I still couldn't tell, but oh, mama, I was in love. I slipped up beside her and started nuzzling the nape of her neck, and then . . . she bit me. That's right, she turned around and bit me on the nose.

Women! Don't understand them, never will. I don't care if they are dogs or squirrels or birds or even Mathilde, they are a species unto themselves.

They flirt, flirt, flirt, flirt, flirt, flirt, flirt, flirt, and then they bite. (Well, Mathilde doesn't bite.) But what is that? Why do women always play so hard to get? I didn't have time to answer that question. I just had to figure that in this case, "hard to get" meant "come on, baby, I want you." So, I went for it.

MOOSE-ISM

THE ONLY THING TO FEAR IS PIT BULLS.

I chased Folie around the yard. She zigged, I zagged. She went right, I went left. She ducked behind the doghouse, I was right behind her. And that's where Mathilde found me, right behind her. Locked together in love's embrace.

Mathilde didn't know what to do. But I did, even though I had never done it before. I was doing it, and I wasn't about to stop doing it for anybody. Mathilde was very upset. We were going to be late for work. She later told me that she considered putting both me and Folie in the car, locked together. But she thought better of it. Folie looked like she was ready to bite someone, and apparently I had a sort of glazed expression on my face. Mathilde threatened to dump water on us, which would have ticked me off to no end.

Quickly though, my youth won out, and it was over before I knew it. Folie and I lay together spent, like Cole and Ashley from The Young and the Restless *when they "reunited" in Spain. Mathilde scooped me up, and put me in the car. I didn't feel much like working, I felt more like having a cigarette, and that was before I started smoking.*

I hoped Folie would be waiting for me when I got back, but she wasn't. We never got together again. I miss her. I think we could have made a life together. But she will always be my first. And because of that, she'll always hold a special place in my heart. About twelve weeks later, she sent me three girls—Miko, Mixie, and Maya. All M names like their dad. They've moved out on their own now. But we still keep in touch. I thought that was really nice of Folie. I always wanted a family.

My second time was with two Corgis and a Pomeranian . . . but that's all you'll be getting from my diary until I'm posthumous. I've got my daughters' feelings to consider.

Fatherhood

I'm a very specific kind of dog, with very specific coloring and spots. Mathilde had been looking around for some time for someone who could be my understudy, but she couldn't find anyone. So she decided I should procreate my own understudy, and along came a femle Jack Russell named Edee (pronounced eee-dee). Edee should have been a good fit; we had the same kind of coloring and all. And she was—a good fit, that is—but our four kids had the wrong spots, so Mathilde didn't keep any of them.

Then along came Enzo. I get proposition letters all the time, which you'll see in the fan mail chapter. Normally, I try to keep my distance from those women, like my mother warned me, but Enzo's mom was something else. She sent me a picture of herself, and well, I couldn't resist. And the result of that "nonresistance" was Enzo, who looks just like me. He's now my understudy, and he's becoming quite a fine young actor in his own right.

Later I met Dreamie at a dog show. And she was. Dreamy, that is.

We got to sniffing each other and really hit it off. Mathilde talked to one of Dreamie's people, and they set up a tête-à-tête for us. Six weeks later, along comes Moosie—another son.

And that's it for my young-uns. I am currently living alone. So, if there are any hot young babes out there, give me a call. All you have to do is sign a pup prenup, and you too can take a ride on the Moose side.

15.
Celebrity Encounters of the Third Kind

Do you ever wonder why celebrities only seem to date other celebrities? Me too. Over the course of the last six years, I've met a lot of them—celebrities, that is. Some are nice, some aren't. Basically, they are like everyone else, except that they have a lot more money than most, and everything they do is watched by somebody else. Well, what's it like to be one of the watched?

Talk Show Hosts
PHIL DONAHUE, SEPTEMBER 1994

It was my first trip to New York, and my first trip first class, and my first talk show with the cast. Phil interviewed me and then I had to do a demonstration of my tricks for the audience. They asked me tons of questions. What is your real name? (Moose.) How old are you? (Not telling.) How do you travel? (Well, first class now.) Who owns you? (Does anybody really own anybody?)

The rest of the cast answered some questions too. But I was

the most articulate. I thought on the whole, it went very well. Phil was a very affable, pleasant host, I'm sorry his show isn't on the air anymore.

DAVID LETTERMAN, SEPTEMBER 1994

When David Letterman found out that I was in New York, he wanted me to come on his show. Kelsey happened to be doing it as well (he's always riding my coattails). Dave (I'm one of the few who can call him that) asked if I knew any stupid pet tricks that we could do together. I told him I didn't have anything stupid, but I was working on a trick where I pretended to lift my back leg. He loved it. So I told him I'd try and get the trick ready for his show.

MOOSE-ISM

NO GOOD TRICK
GOES UNREWARDED.

A few days later, it was show time. As I entered the stage, by myself, the audience burst into a huge round of applause. Then I went over to Dave, as planned, and I lifted my back leg and pretended to pee on him. Well, it brought down the house. Isn't that weird? Pee on somebody's couch, you get yelled at. Pee on the host's leg and you get a standing ovation.

We didn't have time for the usual interview, which was fine by me. Dave makes me nervous. You never know what he's going to say, and sometimes his questions are unnerving. Funny, but unnerving.

As Mathilde and I exited the back door of the Ed Sullivan Theatre,

I had to have a security guard escort me through the throngs of people asking for my autograph and trying to take my picture. All in all, I'd have to say it was a pretty good day.

JAY LENO, 1994

I first went on Jay Leno at the request of Barbara Bush. Yes, the former First Lady of the United States of America. That Barbara Bush. She was going to be on the *Tonight Show* to promote her book about Millie. Yes, the former First Dog of the United States of America. That Millie.

The plan was for me to make a surprise entrance and jump on her lap. And that's what I rehearsed—but not with Mrs. Bush. I rehearsed with a stand-in. When I actually did the bit in front of a live television audience, Barbara was wearing a dress and sitting in such a way that when I jumped on her lap, I bounced off her and almost fell back on the floor. *Très* embarrassing.

She was so sweet about the whole thing though (she's obviously a dog person) that I asked her to sign my copy of the Millie book. She did and I keep it in a treasured place beside my bed. I look at it every night before I go to sleep so I'll often dream of my "Babs."

JAY LENO, THE SECOND TIME

I had been out of commission on *Frasier* for about three months because of a swelling in my ear. Enzo had been substituting for me. Well, Enzo is good—he's my son after all—but he's no me, and NBC was starting to get letters and E-mails from people worried about what had happened to their favorite character on *Frasier.*

Jay was kind enough to have me on his show so that everyone in America could see that I was fine, and that the real Eddie would go on as soon as the swelling went down.

LEEZA

I went on a Christmas shopping spree. I got to buy anything I wanted and then give it to the guys at the Pet Orphans Fund. If you could have seen the looks on their faces when I walked in with my bag full of goodies, it would have brought tears to your eyes.

I was also on the *Sally Jessy Raphael Show* and the *Marilu* (Henner) talk show. They were typical talk shows, and I pulled out my typical bag of tricks. Fortunately, neither of them knew about my secret diary.

LARRY KING IN 1998

For me, the highlight of all the talk shows was when Larry King interviewed us for the celebration of *Frasier*'s 100th episode. Larry wanted to do an interview with the entire cast for the 100th show, but the rest of the cast locked me in a closet to keep me from going.

Well, when they showed up without me, Larry would have none of it. No interview with the *Frasier* cast would be complete without me. Larry came to the set of *Frasier*, and we shot the interview there. (I didn't mention the closet thing.) Larry offered to interview just me, but I insisted that the rest of the cast be part of it. It was our 100th episode, and I've always been about inclusion.

Some of the Actors I've Met

I met Woody Harrelson on my show. He doesn't eat meat, which is something I do not understand, but there's not a nicer person anywhere. We didn't have a lot to do together on the episode, and that was a disappointment to both of us.

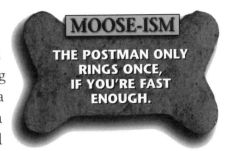

But the time we did spend together was quality.

In 1998, I filmed *My Dog Skip* with Kevin Bacon and my son Enzo. It was so hot in Alabama, where we shot the film, that Mathilde would hold an umbrella over me between takes. Kevin thought that was hilarious, and we really hit it off. We swore to keep in touch after the shoot, but I think he accidentally gave me the wrong phone number because every time I call I get a Thai restaurant in Dallas.

Diane Lane was also in *My Dog Skip*, but I only admired her from a distance. Beautiful women sometimes make me nervous.

I'd always been a big fan of Clint Black's, (although there's never "No Time to Kill" cats). So, when he asked me to make a guest appearance in his music video "Summer's Comin'" I was happy to oblige. Afterwards, he sent me this letter:

October 7, 1994
Dear Moose:

I can't thank you enough for taking the time out of your busy schedule to make an appearance in "Summer's Comin'." I hope you enjoy it as much as I do.

Best regards,
Clint Black
(dictated but not read)

As you can see from the letter, he thought I was brilliant. You have to read between the lines with these country singers. The only thing I found confusing was "dictated but not read." Isn't that kind of like this book I'm writing?

MOOSE-ISM

A DAY WITHOUT A DOGGY TREAT IS LIKE A DAY WITHOUT . . . OH, WHY BOTHER?

Maui (alias Murray from *Mad About You*) and I only worked together once— a photo shoot for the cover of *TV Guide*.

Maui was a collie mix, and he's best known for being able to lie on the couch like a pillow and do nothing. And you know what? Nobody did it better than Maui. I'll miss watching him every week.

Secret Loves

When word got out that I was writing a book, naturally everyone in Hollywood wanted to be in it. I couldn't include everybody, so I sent letters to three of my favorite actresses, asking them for a quote. Here are the responses I got:

from the fabulous Jorja Fox from ER:

Moose and I met at the *Pet Shop*. You know, the talk show on Animal Planet. Moose was striking, confident, and mysterious. He spent the morning making eyes and aggressive advancements, you know the kind [that sniff and snarl, the way the tail moves], at my dog Ali, who was also a guest on the show. It got so heated that Moose and Ali couldn't go to makeup and hair together. And then, he never called. Ali hasn't looked at another Jack Russell since. But occasionally, I do find her curled up under the TV listening longingly for *Frasier* promos. Good luck with the book.

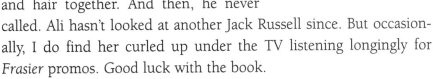

MOOSE-ISM

DOGS ALWAYS TELL THE TRUTH. EVER SEE US BLUSHING?

[It's true. That foxy lady from *ER* had a foxy lady herself. But what can I say? I'm a love 'em and leave 'em pooch.]

from the incredible Jenna Elfman:

He's very talented. He's an inspiration to us all.

[So, are you baby, so are you.]

from one of the funniest people in television, Betty White:

Dearest Moose,

What a thrill to actually be in touch (or almost) with you. It may seem silly at my age to have a really big crush on a celebrity, but it was love at first sight from the very beginning.

With all my heart, you clever devil,
Betty White

[There's nothing silly about it. Love can bloom across the ages.]

16.
The Tabloids: Truth or Fiction?

Okay, over the past six years, I've stood by while lie after lie after lie has been written about me. I couldn't afford to sue these newspaper rags because they have a battery of lawyers that will drag it out for years. But I can answer these false charges and allegations right here, right now, and there ain't nothin' they can do about it.

I'm going to start with the headline, give you the story, and then tell the truth, straight from the doggie's mouth.

Sicko Cuts Off Tail and Mails It to Ex-Girlfriend!

Burlington, VT—Missy, a female Jack Russell terrier, who had once had a brief fling with Moose—Frasier's Eddie the dog—reportedly received a piece of his tail in the mail, as a token of his affection! Missy's owner was appalled. "What happened to flowers?" she asked. When questioned about the incident, Moose denied it vehemently. But before and after pictures show his tail is considerably shorter. Plastic surgeons say that even if he wanted to, there's no chance of reattaching the tail.

What's the big deal? She asked for a lock of my hair, and it happened to come from my tail. And as for those pictures . . . well, forgive me for living, but don't most Hollywood stars have a nip and a tuck every now and then?

A Couple of Gay Blades?

It's been reported by more than one reliable source that Moose (Frasier's Eddie) and Maui (Mad About You's Murray) are more than just pals. They have been spotted playing and biting each other's neck in public, and are frequently seen roughhousing in an intimate fashion. Both actors deny the rumors, but why do they have the same telephone number?

MOOSE-ISM

I DON'T HAVE A BIG EGO. I'M THAT PERFECT.

There is absolutely no truth to the rumors about Murray and me. We're pals, nothing more. So we like to roughhouse a little. We both competed in Greco-Roman wrestling in high school, and it kind of brings back old times. And yeah, okay, there have been a few occasions when we both had a little too much to drink at a big Hollywood party, and Murray ended up staying over. But nothing happened. I swear. Nothing! I didn't even know dogs could be gay.

Tabloid Prediction

Look for handsome canine actor Moose to retire from show biz very soon . . . to run for political office in his home state of Florida.

Sorry to disappoint all my Florida fans, but I believe actors should stay out of politics, and politicians should stay out of acting.

Frasier Star Visited By Sign

Hollywood, CA—Mathilde de Cagny, trainer and acting coach to Moose, who plays Eddie the dog on the television show Frasier, *was surprised one day when Moose, after doing a particularly difficult trick, refused to eat his doggy treat. Instead of eating it, informed sources say, he put it on his pillow in his trailer and just stared at it, the way he stares at Frasier on the show.*

When Mathilde and others approached the pillow, Moose would growl at them, warning them to go away. Mathilde was upset, she didn't know what to do. Moose was needed on the set, but he wouldn't budge, and no one could get close enough to see what he was looking at. Finally, Mathilde threw a blanket over him so she could put him in his crate. When she returned to look at the doggy treat, she was as amazed as Moose had been. Instead of being shaped like a bone, one end was shaped like the head of Christ. She had it framed, and now people come from all over the world to view the holy relic as a cure for fleas.

That is the most ridiculous thing I've ever heard. It was the head of Colonel Sanders. And I ate it.

Moose's Wacky Handout to Peculiar Fan

The nutty canine knows no bounds when it comes to pleasing his fans. "I never would have believed it if I hadn't seen it with my own eyes," says a witness to the exchange that followed a fundraising event at Grauman's Chinese Theatre in Los Angeles.

"A woman asked for his autograph, but neither she nor Moose was carrying a pen. So, without hesitating a second, Moose shook his collar off, grabbed it in his mouth, and offered it to the woman as a souvenir."

The friendly terrier has a reputation for being generous to fans and children. He has given generously to many.

"Moose has his faults," says animal expert and gossip columnist Matt Drudge, "but he has always been in touch with ordinary people." He goes on to say that "offering the woman his collar may have seemed like an odd gesture to an outsider, but those in the know will tell you that it's worth way more than an autograph."

"That collar could fetch in the thousands at a memorabilia auction. I wish he'd have given it to me," confessed Matt.

Actually, this is true. The only odd thing about the whole event was that after I gave her the collar, the woman put it around her own neck and started barking, while being led away on all fours by her leather-clad boyfriend.

TV Pooch Makes Ten Worst-Dressed List!

Okay, people, give me a break here. I can have a bad hair day like the rest of you. But when your hair covers ninety-nine percent of your entire body, then it's a really bad hair day.

Big Feud Over Tell-all Tome

Word on the street is that Enzo, child of and frequent stand-in for Moose, TV's Eddie, is writing a tell-all book about growing up with his abusive father.

"It wasn't that he hit us or anything," says Enzo, *"but he was never very supportive. We would want to play catch, or chase squirrels, but he always insisted on showing us how to do it. He had all the fun, while we watched. We never got any paws-on experience. That's no way to teach a child."*

Enzo goes on to say that Moose used to make the rest of the family wait while he ate. He had to be the first one out in the yard every morning, so he could pee on everything before anyone else could. *"It was horrible and demeaning,"* says Enzo. *"I couldn't wait to get away from him."*

MOOSE-ISM

ASK NOT WHAT YOUR COUNTRY CAN DO FOR YOU, BUT WHAT *YOU* CAN DO FOR *ME*.

Enzo's brother, Moosie, has a different story. He thought his father was loving and protective. *"Yes, he was overly controlling, but that was because he didn't want any one of us to get hurt."* Moosie has begged Enzo not to write the withering tome, but Enzo is insisting that this story must be told.

"Everybody thinks my dad is 'Mr. Perfect.' He's so well behaved. Does what he's told. Always charming and doing funny little bits on his big television show. Well, let me tell you, Dad was and always will be the Alpha Dog, and growing up with him was no picnic."

First of all, I don't believe that just because you practice a little discipline with your kids, it's abuse. And secondly, the next time I see him, he's kibble.

Is Star's Ruff Too Rough for Ma Bell?

On the set of his new flick My Dog Skip, *canine actor Moose zipped back to his doggy trailer between takes and used those doggy paws to dial*

1–900–RUFF–LUV, where he burned up the phone lines with some sexy growling and heavy breathing. What Moose didn't realize is that his wireless mike was still on, and the entire set was listening in on his sizzling exchange. When Moose came out of his trailer, the entire crew burst out laughing. The newly nicknamed "Hound Dog" was embarrassed. It's going to be a long time before Moose lives this one down.

MOOSE-ISM

ALL THINGS COME TO HE WHO WAITS, IF HE GETS CAST IN A SUCCESSFUL TELEVISION SHOW THAT WINS EMMYS AND EARNS HIM WHEELBARROWS FULL OF CASH WHILE HE WAITS.

That tape is now available for $19.95 at www.moose.com. If you can't beat 'em, make money off 'em.

Dog Bites Reporter, Reporter Bites Back—In Court!

A paparazzo known as Jimmy the Flash has filed a lawsuit against celebrity pooch Moose for biting him in the butt.

According to Los Angeles's courthouse records, the incident took place outside of famous Beverly Hills eatery Spago, while Moose was waiting for his limo.

As one bystander reported, "The incident began innocently enough. Moose came out of the restaurant, and the usual autograph seekers surrounded him. And Moose was delightful, signing his paw print to anything put in front of him. But then this photographer appeared from nowhere, and started snapping pictures. Moose growled at him to move on, but the photographer kept snapping. So, Moose bit him. In the butt!"

Is Moose the next Sean Penn? That's what Jimmy the Flash is wondering. "It was the same thing with Sean," says Jimmy. "One minute he'd be the nicest guy in the world, and the next thing you know he bites you in the butt. What is it with these stars? We're the ones who made them stars in the first place! And now, while Moose gets to go back to his hoity-toity mansion, I have to eat standing up."

Against my lawyer's wishes, I am going to comment on this. Jimmy the Flash did not make me a star, and neither did any other of those blood-sucking, parasitic tabloid reporters. If I'm a star, I became one through hard work, some lucky breaks, and a huge amount of talent, not because somebody put me on the cover of a magazine. And just because I'm in the public life doesn't mean I have to give up my private one. Jimmy the Flash has been following me for years: hiding out in the bushes near my house, going through my trash, even taking pictures of my kids. He's talked to every old girlfriend I've ever had, and anybody else who ever had a grudge against me. It's haunting and disturbing, and frankly, I'd bite him again. I don't care what it cost.

Alien Impersonating Popular TV Pet

Eddie is a fraud. According to the National Union of Telepathics Society (NUTS), Moose, who plays Eddie on the television show Frasier, *is not a dog at all, but a being from another planet.*

Robert Blum, president of NUTS, claims Moose was sent to Earth in preparation for an invasion. "He's a

MOOSE-ISM

THE PROBLEM WITH MONEY IS THAT THERE'S NEVER ENOUGH OF IT. OH, YOU HAVE ENOUGH? NEED A PET?

spy, nothing more, nothing less. He's an alien. He should be on the TV show Third Rock From The Sun *instead of* Frasier."

NUTS believe that the television provides extraterrestrials a two-way signal into the homes of all Americans. "The aliens use the signal to look for our weaknesses, while at the same time they fill our minds with propaganda, teaching us to love all small furry four-legged creatures—particularly Jack Russell terriers. Moose acts so adorable to get Earthlings to open their hearts to him. Once everyone in the world wants a Jack Russell terrier, the aliens will invade our planet in the form of Jack Russells and, like the Trojan horse, they will be naively taken into every home in America. They will be there, loving us and licking us and doing tricks for us, while all the time they will be spying and looking for our weaknesses. When the day of reckoning comes, they will take over the world."

MOOSE-ISM

FAMILIARITY BREEDS CONTEMPT. BUT IT'S MORE FUN TO BREED WITH THE UNFAMILIAR.

If I were really an alien, do you think I'd tell you?

My Own Brush With Death

BY MOOSE (TV'S EDDIE)

(In another example of one of the many shocking cases of celebs being victims of crime, we were able to obtain the exclusive story of Moose's, Frasier's Eddie the dog, very own brush with death. The following story is in his own words.)

I was walking with Mathilde. She likes to get out, and I don't mind taking her. We were walking in a park area, not a dog park, but there were a few trees and the occasional bush to pee on. I was on a leash because of that stupid leash law they have in Los Angeles. We're organizing to have that law repealed, but that's another story.

It was a long leash, so I had plenty of room to roam around. I had marked the mailbox, and sprayed an area around an oleander where a Doberman had sprayed earlier. It was a good day. I had gotten messages from other dogs and left a series of my own pee-mail.

We were headed back to the car, when out of the blue, a huge brown-and-black dog—part mastiff, part bloodhound, a nasty specimen with brown and black spots, a square face, and jaundiced yellow eyes—ambushed me. He grabbed me by the neck in a death grip, and wouldn't let go. I could do nothing.

Mathilde was alone. No one else was around to stop the other dog, so she grabbed that dog's neck and shook him as hard as she could. But he wouldn't let go. He just squeezed harder and harder. I thought, this is it. I'm going to die!

My life flashed before my eyes and I thought about . . .

How the people will mourn.

The other great ones who have been cut down in their prime: James Dean, Marilyn Monroe, Elvis.

All the women in all the world that I'm never going to get to know. And who will never get to know me.

As I saw the white light, and could feel myself being drawn to it, Mathilde finally got the dog to let me go. She picked me up, and started hitting the other dog with the leash. She made her way back to the car. Got in and locked the door.

I was in shock. Shaking. I had two very deep holes in my neck, as if a vampire had bitten me. Mathilde drove like a madwoman to the emer-

gency room. When we arrived at the vet, it was a touch and go situation. The vet just stood over me, shaking his head. But he was able to stitch me up, and I survived. He said I was lucky. The punctures were really close to my jugular vein—a quarter of an inch closer, and I would have been puppy chow.

17.
Dear Moose

Since I get bags of fan mail every week, I wanted to take the opportunity to share with you some of the many letters I've gotten over the years and answer some of your most frequently asked questions.

The first letter comes from G.P. in Oberlin, Ohio.

Dear Moose,
What is your real name?

Dear Slow One,
It's Moose. One word. Moose. Like Cher, or Madonna, or Sting. Only, I can't sing, and I still have my own hair. So, like Madonna.

The next letter comes from J.K. in Portland, Oregon.

Dear Moose,
How old are you?

Dear Nosey,
You don't ask an actor that kind of question.

L.F. in Los Angeles wrote this letter to NBC:

Dear Sirs,
I am in love with Eddie. The only reason I watch Frasier (don't tell the cast) is because I love Eddie. I told my friends I wanted to get a picture of Eddie and they told me to write to the studio. After seeing the story on Hard Copy (such a trashy show) about Eddie I now realize that I am not the only one who thinks Eddie is a cute dog. Would you please send me a picture of Eddie? If you only have pictures with the other cast members it is acceptable. Thank you.

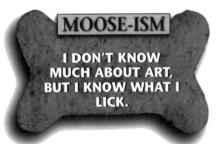

MOOSE-ISM

I DON'T KNOW MUCH ABOUT ART, BUT I KNOW WHAT I LICK.

Dear Gracious Lady,
Here is your picture. And I have taken the trouble to black out the other members of the cast with a magic marker.

From A.H. in Wilmington, North Carolina:

Dear Moose,
Were you always funny?

Dear First Intelligent Question I've Gotten So Far,
Yes.

C.S. of Great Barrington, Massachusetts writes:

Dear Moose,
What kind of dog are you?

Dear Cheapskate,
Buy the book and find out for yourself.

From B.J. in Cleveland, Ohio:

Dear Moose,
What kind of dog food do you eat?

Dear President of Bil Jac,
Next time you should not send in your question on company letterhead. However, thank you for giving me the opportunity to plug your Bil Jac Dog Food and Bil Jac Liver Treat snacks. I love them. They are delicious.

Honestly, though, I'll eat anything. (Talk about biting the hand that feeds you.) As a matter of fact, in 1994 after a Christmas hiatus (hiatus is the hoity-toity word that people in the industry use when they really mean vacation) my daughter Miko and I were making our entrance onto the *Frasier* stage. As usual, we were looking around for bits and pieces of popcorn, and other edible tidbits, and we found a bonanza. There were these pellets everywhere. And they were delicious.

MOOSE-ISM

WHAT EXACTLY ARE THE "DOG DAYS OF SUMMER"? BECAUSE I THINK I'M INSULTED.

What we didn't know was that someone had put rat poison out over the holidays, and that's what we were eating. Fortunately, Mathilde noticed what it was, and rushed us to see our vet, Dr. Jim Peddie. We had to have our stomachs pumped. Which was awful. But it saved our lives. Which was good. It was a very close call. And it just goes to show you, if it's edible, I'll eat it.

A letter from M.T. in London, England:

Dear Moose,
I think you're the best thing in Frasier *and that's saying something. Please send me a photo.*
P.S. You should have your own series.

Dear Insightful One,
I couldn't agree with you more.
P.S. You should have your own network.

From J.S. in New York, New York:

Dear Moose,
Does Kelsey really hate you?

Dear Troublemaker,
No. He does not. In fact, Kelsey loves dogs. He has a bunch of his own and he makes a very good dog scratcher. He definitely knows the spot where I am most ticklish. I even think he enjoys it when I clean his ears. And if you want to know a little secret, Kelsey's breath smells like popcorn.

J.P from Shenandoah writes:

Dear Betty,
How much money do you make per episode?

Dear Hard of Hearing,
Betty!? My name is Eddie, not Betty. And to answer your question, I make $*,***,*** per episode. Plus, I get ** percent of the net profits, and ** percent of the gross merchandising. It comes to about $*** million a year.

N.H. of Wayne, Pennsylvania writes:

Dear Cast of Frasier,
I am a devoted fan of your show. I find the show to be humorous and enlightening. I make sure that I am home every Thursday to watch it. One of my favorite characters is Eddie. He is the neatest dog I have ever seen and he adds so much to the show. I thought it would be an interesting idea

to do a show around Eddie—maybe his perspective of the events that occur around him.

I would like to be sent an autographed photo of Eddie and some information about his breed and training. I would be very appreciative.

Dear Genius,

Enclosed is a packet about Jack Russell terriers. Also, would you like a job writing on our show?

A letter from K.B. in Hockessin, Delaware:

Dear Eddie (Moose),

Hello! How are you? You are so cute. I love to watch your show. I think it should be named Eddie instead of Frasier. You are the real star!

I have a yellow Labrador retriever named . . . blah, blah, blah, blah, blah, blah, blah, blah . . . ah, here we go . . . You are a great actor. I think it is horrible that you were not nominated for an Emmy. My favorite episodes were when you had puppies, and when you wore your Santa suit. If you are ever in Delaware, we have plenty of dog biscuits and food.

Dear Talks Too Much About Your Own Dog,

Thank you so much for your kind letter. It is unlikely that I will be in Delaware in the near future, but you can mail dog biscuits, you know. And I am not too proud to accept presents from fans. As a matter of fact, I feel it is my duty as a celebrity to accept them. Past presents have included, but not been limited to:

1. *A leather biker jacket with matching cap.*

2. *A green and brown winter coat.*

3. *A Santa Claus outfit, not unlike the one I wore in the show.*

4. *A bathrobe from the Four Seasons Hotel.*

5. *Winter snow boots.*

6. *T-shirts.*

7. *A Frasier jacket with my name embroidered on the front in gold.*

8. *Numerous hankies for Christmas, Easter, and the Fourth of July.*

Other items I am in need of:

1. *A DVD player with a flat screen HDTV.*

2. *A '99 Jaguar XK8 convertible.*

3. *A Malibu beach house.*

4. *A Lear jet, or at least a time-share in one.*

5. *Ten thousand shares of Microsoft for my pension plan.*

6. *A ski boat.*

7. *A private car on the Orient Express.*

8. *And the top floor of the St. Pierre in New York City.*

Failing all that, I could use a new blankie.

To the NBC network:

Gentlemen:

We love Eddie the dog. He is the reason we watch the show. In fact, do you really need those other characters on Frasier? Talk, talk, talk, that's all they do.

Please, more time—much more—to Eddie. He's hilarious. He makes the days a little better, the air a little sweeter, and our lives a little brighter. Snoopy, move over.

Anonymoose

From J and J in Washington, D.C.:

Dear Moose,
Why does your tongue always stick out?

Dear Smarty Pants,
You mean like how I'm doing it at you now?
Actually, at a very young age, I started to chew on everything in sight, most of the time out of frustration and impatience. By doing this, I damaged my teeth, wearing them down until they could no longer contain my tongue. In fact, during the summer, the tip of my tongue gets sunburned when I fall asleep in the sun.

From P.R., in Lakewood, Colorado:

Dear Eddie (a.k.a. Moose),
I love watching you on Frasier. You are so adorable and intelligent-looking!
Do you ever make appearances across the country? It may sound crazy, but I would love to be able to meet you. I think having a Jack Russell terrier as a pet would be wonderful. I live in a small apartment and can't have pets, but someday I hope to have a schnauzer and a sweet pup like yourself.
Could you please send me a photo? To keep me company until I can get

a real dog. I would especially like it if the photo could include Jane Leeves. Even better if it included just your paws and Jane Leeves's feet.

Dear Bizarro,
What?

_____

From M.J. in Chicago:

Dear Moose,
How high can you jump?

MOOSE-ISM

(NOTE TO GEORGE LUCAS) I WOULD BE EXCELLENT IN ONE OF THE NEW _STAR WARS_ MOVIES.

Dear Six-Foot-Six, 216 lbs., Retired African-American Basketball Player,
I can jump six feet high. I love Chicago. And I'm a huge fan of the Chicago Bulls. I have cousins in North Carolina and I also happen to be looking for a Nike sponsorship, if you have any contacts in that area.

_____

And finally, a few of the propositions I've gotten from some hot-looking babes . . .

From S.D in Seattle, Washington:

Dear Moose, alias Eddie Crane,
I am your biggest fan! I can't wait until Thursdays at 9:30 P.M. when I get to watch your show. It is my favorite. I watch you faithfully every week.
It would be a dream come true if I were to get a chance to meet you. I know that even though your show takes place in Seattle, where I live, you probably film in Hollywood. But, if you ever get up this way, I would love to have you over for dinner. I prefer a good steak, but I also make a lovely lean chicken if you happen to be on a strict diet like most of you stars often

are. Also, I have a great little place in my parents' backyard that's perfect for summer dining!

Enclosed are two photos taken of me. I hope you think I am as cute as I find you.

And from C.M. in Los Vegas, Nevada:

Moose/Eddie,

My family is writing to wish you a happy holiday and tell you we enjoy your acting. If you ever want a girlfriend, I'm as cute as you are. I love to roll on my back on the furniture and [censored]. I love to carry things in my mouth and do other things like [censored]. I am interested in raising a family. Enclosed is my picture.

And finally from W. in Skokie, Illinois:

Dear Eddie:

Hi there, big guy. I hope you like my pinup photo. My name is Widget. I'm a female, rough-coated, two-year-old Jack Russell terrier. I live in a suburb of Chicago. If you are ever in Chicago, stop by and see me sometime. I've got some tricks that will curl the hair on your chinny-chin-chin.

Dear Ladies,

Please. There is only so much Moose to go around. I appreciate your interest, but right now I'm in a serious relationship. Don't give up hope, though—you know how long "serious" relationships last in Hollywood.

18.
My Way

One day an older lady was waiting in line to have her picture taken with me. As we arrived, she said that she had waited in line for only two celebrities in her entire life: me and Frank Sinatra.

Needless to say, I was surprised, and honored. But when I thought about it, I realized that Frank and I have a lot in common.

1. We both started as nobodies and had to work our way to the top.

2. We both succeeded beyond our wildest dreams and are adored by millions of fans.

3. And, finally, we both did it "Our Way."

So, in honor of Frank, and to sum up how I feel about my life, my career, and the writing of this book, I have adapted his signature song for my own.

Moose's Way

And now, the end is near;
So I must write the final pages.
I've made my views so clear
In hope they'll last throughout the ages.

I've traveled near and far
And marked each hydrant on the highway
Then I became a star
I did it my way.

My fame, it shocked the cast
(As you could tell from that first chapter)
Who knew I'd learn so fast
To steal the scenes and hog the laughter.

Disheveled looks, a simple stare,
That got me known from Maine to Norway
A mutt, covered with hair
I did it my way.

Yes, there were times, I thought I'd fail
Between my legs, you'd find my tail.
When things got tough, when all looked stark,
I lost my bite, but not my bark.
When life got tough, I just said, "Ruff,"
And did it my way.

To Jane and John and Dave
To Kelsey too, Mathilde and Peri
With you, I could be brave
You held my paw when things got scary.

My thanks to all who helped
Me reach each goal along the byway.
We had good times, we laughed—
And did it my way.

For what I've done, is done by few.
I've fame that others wish they knew.
If you work hard, you can be great.
Success is not a quirk of fate.
If you believe, it's not too late,
To do it my way!

Early me

I ~~oughta be~~ **am** in pictures

My first kid, Enzo

Me & my son — puppy love

Mom

Dad

Useless military training

Unwinding on a camping trip in Ojai

Me & Mathilde on my yacht—like Ari & Jackie O.

Mathilde setting up a sleepover with my girlfriend Edee

Learning lines

PHOTO BY MARSHA NORDBYE

Teaching an old
dog new tricks

COURTESY OF PARAMOUNT

A scene with Kelsey (Notice how he's trying to upstage me.)

My first death scene

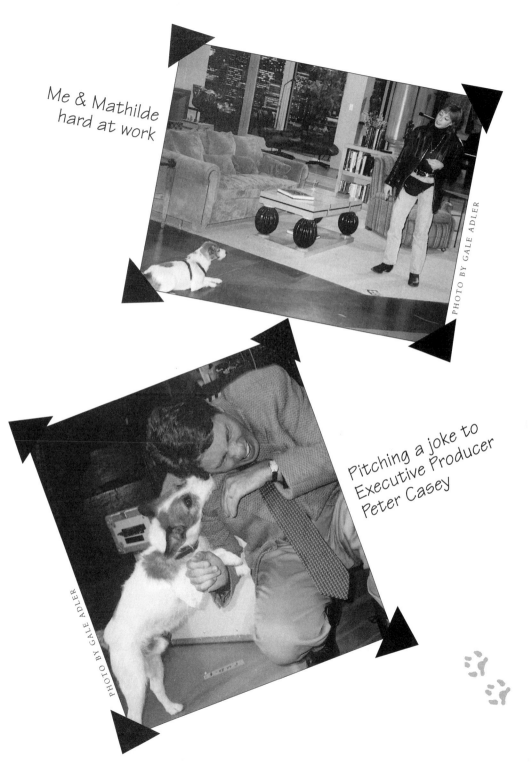

Me & Mathilde hard at work

PHOTO BY GALE ADLER

Pitching a joke to Executive Producer Peter Casey

PHOTO BY GALE ADLER

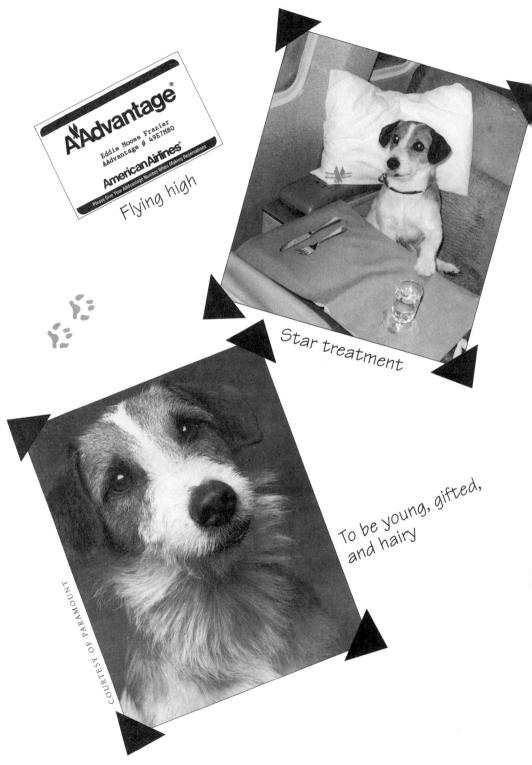

AAdvantage®

Eddie Moose Frazier
AAdvantage # 49E7M80

AmericanAirlines®

Please Give Your AAdvantage Number When Making Reservations

Flying high

Star treatment

To be young, gifted, and hairy

COURTESY OF PARAMOUNT

EDDIE
THE DOG

The **Tonight** SHOW
WITH **JAY LENO**

Me with one of my poker buddies

My newest family